The Teaching of History in Primary Schools

Implementing the Revised National Curriculum

Second Edition

Hilary Cooper

David Fulton Publishers

London

David Fulton Publishers Ltd
2 Barbon Close, London WCIN 3JX

First edition published in Great Britain by David Fulton Publishers in 1992,
reprinted in 1994, as *The Teaching of History*

Second edition published in 1995, as *The Teaching of History in Primary Schools*

Note: The right of Hilary Cooper to be identified as the author of this work
has been asserted by her in accordance with the Copyright, Designs and
Patents Act 1988.

Copyright © Hilary Cooper

British Library Cataloguing in Publication Data

A catalogue record for this book is available from the British Library

ISBN 1-85346-403-1

Typeset by The Harrington Consultancy Ltd
Printed in Great Britain by the Cromwell Press, Melksham

Contents

Introduction

The first edition of *The Teaching of History* aimed to show primary school teachers how, in a basic, practical way, the National Curriculum for history, which was introduced in 1991, might be implemented, developed, evaluated and ultimately modified by teachers who were confident but not uncritical. The 1995 revision of the National Curriculum was the result of extensive consultation in the light of teachers' experience. This second edition reviews what has been achieved in the teaching of history in the primary school since it became a required dimension of the curriculum and how this might be built upon in imaginative and creative ways to reflect the framework of the Revised History Order.

In reflecting on what has been achieved in the past four years, it is salutary to remember that the history curriculum was introduced against a background of heated debate about the nature of history in education and whether pupils, particularly young children, could or should be involved in the processes of historical thinking. Often the debate was represented as a polarisation of 'facts' as opposed to the 'whys' and 'ifs' of learning history. Pamphlets from the Centre for Policy Studies (Beattie, 1987) appeared to echo Mr Gradgrind in *Hard Times*:

> Facts. Teach these boys and girls nothing but facts. Facts alone are what is needed in life. Plant nothing else and root out everything else . . . he seemed a galvanizing apparatus, charged with a grim mechanical substitute for the tender young imaginations that were to be stormed away.
>
> (Dickens, 1854)

The *History Workshop Journal* and Ruskin College, Oxford, sponsored heated debates (1989, 1990) on a range of such issues. The History Curriculum Association was set up by academic historians to promote a traditional approach to school history. The Historical Association caused an outcry with its paper 'History in the Core Curriculum' (1987), which recommended sixty chronological topics for pupils from five to sixteen. However, after two rounds of eight lively and well-attended regional conferences in 1987 and 1988, a consensus was achieved amongst teachers in the Historical Association on the essential interaction of process and context, on criteria for defining these, and on the need for continuity and progression in developing and evaluating children's historical understanding. The structure of the National Curriculum for history reflected this achievement in that the content of the History Study Units was selected, taught and evaluated by teachers through the processes set out in the attainment targets. For the first time, it enabled all children to learn history in an increasingly complex way through enquiry and active involvement; it offered a framework for the development of Bruner's spiral curriculum in history (1963, 1966).

For many teachers and children this created a new dimension in the primary curriculum. Although the Plowden Report (1967) had advocated a broad and rich curriculum, much otherwise excellent practice during the last twenty years had echoed the emphasis placed by Bruner and Piaget on direct and concrete experiences; history had often been seen as remote and abstract, concerned with the affairs of adults and so not central to the experiences of young children, and too difficult for them to become actively involved in. The limited amount of research undertaken into young children's ability to understand the past had done little to dispel this idea, for reasons which will be discussed later. Consequently, although there had been some examples of excellent practice (Blyth, 1982, 1988; DES, 1989), history had not been widely taught in primary schools, and when it was taught, it had often been based on television programmes and on copying from poor text books (DES, 1978, 1991; HMI Wales, 1989). There had been no clear aims, in terms of knowledge, skills and attitudes, and no consistent approach to planning and assessment.

During the last four years teachers have been under often intolerable pressures, but have shown themselves to be amazingly resilient. They have been over-burdened with finding ways of implementing, assessing and recording in core curriculum areas, and superimposed on this, have had to absorb new content and ways of structuring it in all the foundation subjects. Yet they have been optimistic, prepared to take risks, have a go and learn through doing so, for there were no blueprints or role models.

In history, the sea-change in four years has been amazing. In schools all over the country we find school museums, displays of 'old things', presentations of local and family history investigations, pictures and models recording visits to sites, museums, galleries and Living History Reconstructions. These are often projects which teachers, particularly at key stage 1, embarked upon reluctantly but discovered how enjoyable and appropriate they could be. Gradually teachers have taken history into account in curriculum and classroom organisation and management, and related it to their existing understanding of how children learn.

The newly secure position of primary history has meant that teachers have, for the first time, been able to draw on a variety of sources of support. There has been a massive response from publishers who competed energetically to produce materials of all kinds which support the teaching of history in the primary school. Books, posters, slides, replica sources, audio and video tapes, have been designed to develop progression in children's historical thinking. Organisations such as English Heritage, the National Trust and museum education departments have developed a wealth of materials, suggestions and experiences linked to the National Curriculum. The Historical Association has extended its publications to cover gaps which exist in the commercial market.

A continuum of shared experience between schools and institutions of higher education has been strengthened through the resourcing of in-service courses and National Curriculum Council projects which investigated the kinds of thinking young children are capable of, for example in understanding concepts of time, or why interpretations of the past may vary, which have been disseminated in a range of publications (NCC, 1993a,b). The developing and productive partnership between higher education, research and schools is also represented in the Nuffield History Primary Project, based at the University of Exeter. The aim of this is for university tutors to work with schools to investigate and share the ways in which history can be taught and assessed at key stages 1 and 2, through enjoyable, creative evidence-based activities.

The main criticism of the history National Curriculum identified in the Dearing Review of 1994 was that there was too much prescribed content and that the assessment structure was fragmented and cumbersome. As a result, content has been reduced, and planning and assessment procedures modified. It has been recognised that teachers' professional judgement is essential in developing a curriculum which is coherent, which takes into account progression, balance, breadth and depth, and reflects the needs of individual schools, their pupils and localities.

Education, like history is a dynamic process, and responding to the new challenge raises many questions as well as opportunities. With the implied emphasis, in the current climate, on basic skills and a notional forty-five hours of history each year, the recently established position of history in the primary curriculum remains fragile. If it is not again to become marginalised in the process of curriculum restructuring, it is essential that we have an articulate rationale for its importance and a clear idea of how it may be related to the rest of the curriculum, building on the experience of the past few years.

The second edition of *The Teaching of History* aims to support that process. The structure of the book is the same as in the first edition although each chapter has modifications which reflect changes in the content and structure of the revised curriculum, the increased experience of teachers in planning history topics, and new resources available to support this. Chapter 1 discusses the nature of historical thinking which underpins History in the National Curriculum. Chapter 2 gives an updated overview of research which investigates the kinds of thinking in history which young children may be capable of. Chapter 3 describes the structure of the revised History Order and the decisions involved in creating a coherent curriculum, then goes on to suggest how this may be done. Case studies in Chapter 4 show how planning for the 1991 history curriculum can be modified to bring it in line with the revisions. In Chapter 5 the description of a residential in-service course for teachers on the seventeenth century, which is no longer essential content, has been replaced by a case study of work undertaken over a term by students working in collaboration with teachers of key stage 1 children in a number of schools to organise a role-play day in a Victorian house. Chapter 6 outlines research undertaken as a class teacher to investigate the effects of teaching strategies based on discussion of sources.

CHAPTER 1

Historical Thinking

Before history became a required part of the primary curriculum, history books for children did not take into account that, from the very beginning children are able, in a simple but genuinely historical way, to grapple with the problems that lie at the heart of the discipline and that they should so do in increasingly complex ways (Bruner, 1966; Lawton, 1975; Pring, 1976). Often books made generalised and stereotpyical statements and gave no indication of the sources on which these were based or of the areas of uncertainty in interpreting sources which influence any description, account or explanation of the past. Children were usually given a single perspective of the past and not helped to see why different people, at different times, create different interpretations which may be more or less valid. The concepts of time and change, motive, cause and consequence, similarity and difference were rarely developed.

> After they had been there for four hundred years, the Romans went away. Their homes in Italy were being attacked by fierce tribes and every soldier was needed. The Britons were sad when they went, for they had no soldiers of their own to protect them from the sea-raiders who were growing bolder in their attacks upon the coast.
>
> (Unstead, 1964, p. 42)

(For current research on causation, and children's understanding of the reasons why the Romans conquered Britain see Dickinson and Lee (1994) referred to in Chapter 2.) Illustrations of artefacts were often presented as curious remnants rather than as rich sources from which a range of possible deductions may be made about the people who used them, and how their lives may have been influenced by them. 'Main events' and 'famous people' were listed at the back of a book simply because they happened, without apparent significance, and without conveying the idea that historians weave them together into accounts of the past, that they select and interpret them, and that this is why accounts may differ.

Children's active learning was often assumed to occur through 'Things to Do' at the end of a chapter, but this rarely involved a reconstruction based on real historical evidence, a real building or an archaeological site, and the inevitable questions this would raise. It is more likely to suggest that you 'Make model Viking ship from stiff card or paper as shown below . . .' (Mitchell and Middleton, 1967, p. 88). Alternatively, children were asked to 'Pretend you are a merchant living in Saxon times and tell of your adventure', which presupposes an understanding of attitudes, values and a social structure quite different from our own, or else invites anachronism and identification and so inhibits the development of true historical understanding. (Dickinson and Lee (1994) are also investigating young children's understanding of motive in the context of Anglo-Saxon oath-taking. This research is referred to in Chapter 2.)

Secondary sources for children were often written in unnecessarily obscure language.

> Drake is the most famous mariner in English history. He is renowned for his adventurous exploits as well as his enterprising skill in establishing the English navy as the country's main national weapon.
>
> (Famous Sailors, 1970)

Yet history is not only concerned with great events or famous men. It encompasses all aspects of the lives of the men, women and children in a society. Historians attempt to find out about them through asking particular kinds of questions of whatever traces of the past remain.

THE CONTENT OF HISTORY

As David Thomson (1969) explained, history has developed over the last two hundred years from chronicles of unrelated events into a discipline which aims to interpret different kinds of evidence in order to understand societies in the past. Its content is diverse: social, economic, constitutional, aesthetic. It may be concerned with individuals, institutions or groups. Philip Phenix (1964) saw history, with religion and philosophy, as forming a 'Realm of Meaning' which unites all other kinds of thinking. The National Curriculum takes account of this breadth of content.

It is the questions historians ask, however, and the ways in which they answer them, that distinguish history as a discipline. History is concerned with the causes and effects of change over time; with the ways in which, and the reasons why, societies in the past were different from ours, and what caused them to change. Historians investigate the past by interpreting traces of the past, the evidence. They interpret evidence through a process of deductive reasoning, but evidence is often incomplete, and for this and other reasons, more than one interpretation may be defensible. Producing a range of valid interpretations involves thinking which we may call 'historical imagination'. A wide and perceptive range of valid interpretations may eventually lead to an understanding of why people in the past may have thought, felt and behaved differently from us. Historical enquiry also depends on concepts which are, in varying degrees, peculiar to history. In this chapter, each of these aspects of historical thinking will be considered in turn. It is important to remember that they interact with each other in the process of finding out about the past.

THE PROCESSES OF HISTORICAL ENQUIRY

Making inferences about the past from evidence

There are many kinds of historical evidence: oral history, artefacts, pictures and photographs, maps, statistics, writing. Written evidence is wide-ranging: documents, laws, tombstone inscriptions, diaries, newspaper accounts, contemporary literature. Making historical inferences involves forming arguments about the significance of a piece of evidence: what does it tell us about the society that produced it? How was it made? Why? What was it used for? By whom? Where was it found? Are there others? . . . and so on.

Superior examples of Roman shoes found at Vindolanda, the equivalent of shoes made by Gucci or Lobbe today, tell us something about the social and economic structure of the fort. A letter from a first generation 'Dutch' Roman at the fort, written in Latin, asking for underpants and socks from Rome, may tell us about the economic and transport systems of the empire, and the attitudes of Dutch tribes to the cold, clothes and culture.

Since there is a limit to what can be known for certain, a historian must also make inferences which are probabilistic – reasonable guesses about the evidence. The four post-holes in the centre of an Iron Age house plan may be to support the roof (Bersu, 1940), they may surround an open courtyard where animals could be kept (Clarke, 1960), or they may be a free-standing tower for repairing the roof (Harding, 1974).

If the evidence is incomplete, the historian must also be able to tolerate that which can never be known; for example, we do not know how much of a new style of agriculture the Romans introduced to Britain, or how it was related to the old, and so how British communities related to Roman villas, since no examples of Roman field patterns have been identified (Richmond, 1955).

This process of enquiry in interpreting historical evidence was clarified by Collingwood in his autobiography (1939). He proceeded from specific questions about the significance and purpose of objects (whether they were buttons, dwellings or settlements), to their meaning for the people who made them. For instance, he *knew* that a Roman wall from the Tyne to Solway existed. He *guessed* its purpose was to form a sentry wall with parapets as a protection against snipers. He *wanted to know* if there were towers as a defence against trying to land at Bowness or St. Bees, in order to support his guess. A search revealed that towers had been found, but their existence forgotten (because their purpose was not questioned).

Interpreting historical evidence involves not only internal argument, but also debate with others, testing inferences against evidence from other sources and considering other points of view. It means then supporting opinions with arguments, accepting that there is not always a 'right' answer, that there may be equally valid but different interpretations, and that some questions cannot be answered. This kind of thinking is as important to the social, emotional and intellectual growth of young children, as it is necessary in adult society.

Developing historical understanding

Interpreting historical evidence may involve suggesting how something was made, or used, or what it may have meant to people at the time. It may involve explaining a sequence of events or the behaviour of an individual or a group. Evidence is always incomplete. It is a reflection of the feelings and thoughts of the people who created it. Historical evidence is, therefore, often open to a variety of equally valid interpretations. In order to interpret evidence, it is necessary to understand that people in the past may have thought, felt and behaved differently from us, because they lived in societies with different knowledge-bases, belief-systems, views of the world, and different social, political and economic constraints.The disposition to make a variety of suggestions about incomplete evidence, which take into account that people in the past may have thought and felt differently from us, is therefore an integral part of making historical inferences. It has been called 'historical imagination' or 'historical empathy'. However, these terms have led to a great deal of confusion because they have often been regarded as the product of free-floating imagination discrete from interpreting evidence. They have also been confused with projecting oneself into the past, or with identifying or sympathising with people in the past. The historian cannot share the thoughts and feelings of people in the past but can attempt to understand and explain what these may have been. There has been confusion too, because the terms 'historical imagination' or 'empathy' involve a number of subordinate concepts: understanding different points of view in a conflict, the motives of an individual or a group, the values, attitudes and beliefs of another society.

Historians have an implicit understanding of historical imagination, which is usually not adequately articulated. Kitson Clarke (1967) pointed out that 'men's actions can be the subject of detailed research, but what went on in their minds can only be known by inference.' Elton (1970) saw historical imagination as 'a tool for filling in the gaps when facts are not available'. Ryle (1979) saw it as a means of cashing in on the facts and using them: ammunition shortage and heavy rain before a battle cause the historian to wonder about the hungry rifleman and delayed mule trains. Thomas (1983) said that what interests him about the past is what ordinary people thought, felt and believed. Collingwood (1939, p. 7) attempted to clarify the relationship between interpreting evidence and interpreting the thoughts and feelings of the people who made it. He says, for example, that we *know* that Julius Caesar invaded Britain in successive years; we can suppose that his *thoughts* may have been about trade, or grain supply, or a range of other possibilities, and that his underlying *feelings* may have included ambition or career advancement. (Mink (1968) rigorously analysed Collingwood's thinking on this subject in his article 'Collingwood's Dialectic of History'.)

Historians, then, do not question that making deductions about historical evidence involves probabilistic interpretations, and conjectures about thoughts, feelings and beliefs. Their job is not to reproduce the lost world of the past, but to ask questions and to try to answer them.

Nevertheless, it is important to recognise that suppositions about the feelings and thoughts of people who made and used historical evidence have to conform to criteria of validity. There must be no contradictory evidence. It must be assumed that people in the past acted rationally. Inferences must be supported by argument and conform to what else is known of the period. Historians must also attempt to understand what the evidence may have meant to people at the time. What, for example, was the status of a torc, dating from 1000 BC, discovered in a Wiltshire field? 'This may have been a votive offering to a God, or buried as part of a funeral ceremony, or it might have been stored' (Merriman, 1990).

Children can take part in the process of making suggestions about how things were made and used and how the people who used them may have thought and felt. They can be helped to imagine, for example, how it may have felt to do the washing using a copper, a dolly, a scrubber and a flat iron, to go to bed by candlelight, or to wear the clothes of children depicted in an old portrait. They can use parish registers, census records, street directories, old maps and information about daily life from secondary sources to reconstruct the life of a particular family living in a particular house at a given time in the past. They can suggest what life may have been like in seventeenth-century London after reading extracts from Pepys' diary, or how a Roman villa they have visited may have looked when it was first built. But the imaginative conjecture must be rooted in the evidence.

Children must be encouraged to 'go beyond the evidence' because this is central to developing historical understanding. Therefore they must gradually learn through discussion with each other and with their teacher how to make interpretations which are historically valid.

Using historical concepts

Historical evidence can only be interpreted through language. In order to ask questions of evidence, we need to use concepts which are in varying degrees peculiar to history. As Blyth (1990) pointed out, however, lists of historical

Bringing History to Life booklets help teachers to plan activities involving historical enquiries about, for example, the Aztecs (Horton, 1992) or the Assyrians (Oakes, 1994) and the new Occasional Papers deal with matters as varied as the role of the history coordinator in the primary school (Lomas, 1994) and the creation and use of a school museum (Batho, 1994). The Women's History Network is developing materials for key stage 1 which have a female perspective. The Association for the Study of African, Caribbean and Asian Culture and History in Britain, and the Northamptonshire Black History Group have produced materials to support the non-Eurocentric perspectives in teaching history in the National Curriculum, as have small publishers such as Bogle L'Ouverture Press (Huntley, 1993). The National Curriculum Council has published a variety of materials showing how to encourage the processes of historical enquiry (NCC, 1991, 1992, 1993a,b) and SCAA and OFSTED plan to extend these with further examples of pupils' responses. There have also been books for teachers offering ideas at a range of levels for developing children's historical thinking (Andreetti, 1993; Hill and Morris, 1991; Knight, 1991, 1993; Blyth, 1994; Watts and Grosvenor, 1995).

Perhaps the next phase of books for children will encourage them to think critically and analytically through raising questions which are an integral part of the text and illustrations. This will recognise that teachers are now also able to go solo, rather than be propped up by schemes which in many ways deskill them. Excellent examples of such books are in the History Mystery Series of which *Bathtime* (Tanner and Wood, 1993) won the primary section of the *Times Educational Supplement* School Book Award in 1993, and in the Turn of the Century Series also published by A. and C. Black. Perhaps the intermediate stage in moving from schemes to very well-produced 'free-standing' books is represented by the 'I Was There' Series based on carefully researched, extravagant reconstructions, which is published by Bodley Head, and the Dorling Kindersley Eyewitness books which contain excellent photographs of sources. Books in both series are delightful and thought-provoking, and support materials of a very high quality suggest how they may be used effectively in schools.

CHAPTER 2

Historical Thinking and Cognitive Development

In this chapter, we shall examine theories of cognitive development relevant to each aspect of historical thinking: making inferences, historical imagination, and concept development. Research which relates each area to children's thinking in history will also be discussed. Finally, we shall consider the implications of cognitive psychology and research into children's learning in history for the structuring of a history curriculum for young children.

THEORIES OF COGNITIVE DEVELOPMENT RELEVANT TO MAKING HISTORICAL INFERENCES

Piaget posited a sequence in the development of children's thinking encompassing three qualitative stages. This is consistent with the view that children become increasingly able to make inferences about the past from historical sources. Young children, he found, were not able to hold more than one perspective at a time. At the next stage children's thinking was bound by observable reality. At the third stage they were able to hold in mind a range of hypothetical possibilities.

Piaget's research on probability and chance (1951) is based on the manipulation of physical objects, predicting the colour of marbles to be drawn from a bag, or rolled down a tray. However, it is interesting that he found that while young children make no differentiation between chance and non-chance, at a concrete level children show an increasing awareness of what they can know and what they can guess, so that at a formal level, they are able to establish a firm bridge between the certain and the probable.

Piaget's work on language (1926) and on logic (1928) is the most helpful to apply to inferential reasoning in history. Here he sets out a sequence in the development of argument. In *The Language and Thought of the Child* (1926) he says that at the egocentric level, the child is not concerned with interesting or convincing others, and leaps from a premise to an unreasonable conclusion in one bound. Next s/he attempts to communicate intellectual processes which are factual and descriptive, and show incipient logic, but this is not clearly expressed. This leads to a valid statement of fact or description. From this follows 'primitive argument' in which the statement or opinion is followed by a deduction going beyond the information given, but the explanation for the deduction is only implicit. At the next stage, the child attempts to justify and demonstrate his assertion by using a conjunction (since, because, therefore), but does not succeed in expressing a truly logical relationship. Piaget says, in *Judgement and Reasoning in the Child*:

> The young child (7–8) rarely spontaneously uses 'because' or 'although' and if forced to finish sentences using them, uses them as a substitute for 'and then'.
>
> (Piaget, 1928)

The child eventually arrives at 'genuine argument', through frequent attempts to justify his own opinions and avoid contradiction, and as the result of internal debate, he is able to use 'because' and 'therefore' correctly to relate an argument to its premise. Finally, at a formal level, s/he can use not only conjunctions, but also disjunctions, can make implications and consider incompatible propositions.

This pattern in the development of argument has been examined, assessed and modified by subsequent research. Peel (1960) identified a 'describer' stage of unjustified and unqualified statements, a transitional stage of justified hypothesis and a recognition of logical possibilities, and an 'explainer' stage of weighed arguments using abstract propositions.

Nevertheless, young children's ability to make inferences may be greater than Piaget suggested. It often seems to be limited by lack of knowledge or experience, or failure to understand the kind of thinking that is expected. In history it would vary, depending on the nature of the evidence. Piaget and Inhelder themselves (Peel, 1960) found levels of thinking varied according to the nature of the questions asked.

A child's interest and involvement are also important as Beard (1960) showed. Isaacs (1948) found very young children capable of logical argument if they understood how to tackle the problem and were interested in it. Wheeler (Peel, 1960) found that logical thinking can exist from an early age, and that it becomes more complex through increased experience and memory. Piaget's own case studies offer some evidence that comments, suggestions and criticisms make pupils aware of the elements in problem-solving, and can accelerate their progress. Donaldson (1978) examined the dichotomy she recognised between children's capacity for reasoning in informal, everyday situations and Piaget's conclusion that children under seven have little reasoning ability. She found that young children are capable of deductive reasoning, that their problem-solving depends on the extent to which they can concentrate on language, and that language development is related to other non-verbal clues which are also brought to bear in problem-solving. She found that children may encounter difficulties because they do not always select relevant items in problem-solving, are easily distracted, and rarely discuss the meaning of words. She concluded that a child's understanding depends on whether the reasoning stems from the child's immediate concerns or is externally imposed, and also on the child's expectation of what the questioner wants to know. She said, therefore, that young children must be helped to develop their ability to reason and to make inferences as early as possible by recognising the abstraction of language, and by receiving the right kind of help in problem-solving. They must also become aware of the nature of different disciplines.

Psychologists' work on reasoning, then, suggests that young children may be helped to develop arguments about historical evidence if we teach them how. It suggests that we need to provide interesting, memorable learning experiences, ask simple, open-ended questions, and teach appropriate vocabulary.

RESEARCH RELATING PSYCHOLOGISTS' WORK ON MAKING INFERENCES TO CHILDREN'S THINKING IN HISTORY

There have been studies relating Piaget's developmental levels to children's historical thinking. However, they have found that the three levels can be revealed amongst a group of children of almost any age, because the nature of the evidence and the complexity of the questions influences children's level of response. Since the studies have usually involved older children, they are of limited value to primary school teachers. Nevertheless, they have been encouraging in recognising approaches to teaching history which have been successful, in establishing that young children enjoy making inferences about historical evidence, and in focusing attention on the quality of children's thinking rather than simply on fact acquisition.

In the 1960s, children's responses to historical evidence were classified in terms of Piagetian levels by Lodwick (1958 in Peel, 1960, p. 121), Thompson (1962), Peel (1960), Booth (1969), Hallam (1975) and Rees (1976). Lodwick's study is perhaps the most useful to those interested in young children because it involved visual evidence and did not depend on understanding individuals' motives, or on causation. He showed children between seven and fourteen a picture of Stonehenge and asked them three questions, for example: 'Do you think Stonehenge might have been a temple or a fort?' Their answers showed a gradual development from unreason to logic, then the use of supporting evidence, and probabilistic thinking. Eventually, they were able both to support a hypothesis that it was a temple, and also to argue as to why it was not a fort. The answers suggest that the development in reasoning is due, to some extent, to an increase in knowledge. More information might therefore have enabled the children to argue logically at an earlier age.

Thompson (1962) gave a mixed ability class of twelve-year-old boys background information about William the Conqueror, then gave them extracts from the *Domesday Book* and from the *Anglo-Saxon Chronicle*, and asked them why William had the survey carried out. This material is far more complex than that of Lodwick, because it involves written evidence, comparing two sources, and understanding both bias and motive. It also involves understanding a society with different rules. At a preoperational level replies showed misunderstanding of the information. At a concrete level children repeated information given in the chronicle. Formal responses showed awareness of uncertainty and probability, an understanding of the King's insecure position, and of his need not to be cheated of taxes. Piaget's work on rules and motives (1932) showed that by twelve years old, children can understand that rules can be changed, they take account of motive, and see that justice is relative. Piaget says this is achieved through comparing and discussing perspectives. However, Thompson (1962) seems to have found some children operating at a fairly low level because of the abstraction and complexity of the material, and also perhaps because he required a written response.

It is not surprising that Peel (1960) traced the same three Piagetian levels of response amongst a group of junior school children when he asked a far more simple question about a story. He told them the story of King Alfred and the cakes, and asked them, 'Could Alfred cook?' Indeed, this is hardly a historical question and requires no understanding of laws, motive, bias or of another society. Peel found that at seven, children's answers were often illogical ('Yes, he was King', or, 'No, he could fight'). At a concrete level, they would restate evidence in the story, but at a transitional level they may state what might be expected ('I shouldn't think so – at least not as well. He didn't pay attention to the cakes. If he had been a good cook he might have known when they'd be done.'). At a formal level, they may state a possibility not given in the text ('I don't know, because if anyone could cook and had something else on his mind, he might still forget the cakes'). Peel's responses might have been analysed in a more refined way, appropriate to the age-range if his categories had reflected Piaget's sequence in *The Language and Thought of the Child* (1959): egocentric, incipient logic, statements of fact, implicit deduction, incomplete causal relationship, genuine argument.

Booth (1969) constructed tests for thirteen- to fourteen-year-olds, designed to explore the nature of their knowledge of history.They were asked questions about time and change, and about the attitudes, ideas and beliefs represented by three religious buildings of different periods. They were also asked to compare and contrast people, events and photographs of houses from different periods. Booth, too, found that answers fell into three categories: those that had little or no comprehension of the material or the questions, those that referred to the information given but made little attempt to refer to historical material outside the question; and those that showed selection and critical thinking and related their work to other relevant knowledge. Such questions and material could easily be adapted for primary school children, and if related to a unit of study, would most likely receive responses at the two higher levels, although their answers may be different from those of thirteen-year-olds.

It seems that researchers tried to fit their children's responses into Piaget's three bands, irrespective of age-group or material, rather than ask simple, open-ended questions and see what patterns emerged.

It is interesting that Booth found more divergent thinking and flexibility when children were asked questions orally and pupils' questionnaires showed that they enjoyed class discussion, local history studies, and examining pictures, documents and maps, and disliked facts, generalisations and 'essay' writing.

In the 1970s, experiments and strategies were designed to see if children's thinking in history could be accelerated within the Piagetian model, by teaching methods. Hallam (1975) worked with nine- and thirteen-year-olds and Rees (1976) with twelve-year-olds.

Hallam taught 'experimental' classes through active problemsolving in role-play ('Imagine you are Henry VIII and say why you have decided to abolish the monasteries'), through asking questions about Cromwell's diary and discussing passages from historical texts. He found that the classes taught through active problem-solving performed at a higher level than the traditionally taught control group.

Rees (1976) also found that children's thinking skills in history could be developed if they were taught to explain rather than describe, and to be aware of uncertainty and motive, by switching perspective. His classes of twelve-year-olds compared favourably at the end of the term with a control group who were taught in a didactic way. Rees found three levels of response to his fairly complex material. Answers requiring inference were considered to be preoperational if no explanation was given, at a concrete level if only one explanatory reference was given, and at a formal level if all explanatory references were given. Responses to questions requiring pupils to take account of two points of view fell into three categories: those which showed no logic, those which showed increasing quantities of substantiating evidence but only in support of one viewpoint, and those that appreciated two viewpoints.

Dickinson and Lee (1978, p. 82) concentrated on defining historical thinking, rather than Piagetian levels, as the starting point. They made clear for the first time the important distinction between understanding behaviour from a contemporary viewpoint and from the standpoint available to the person at the time. They gave adolescents some of the information available to Jellico before the Battle of Jutland and asked them why he turned back. They traced a sequence in the development of the pupils' understanding that there is a difference between Jellico's point of view and that of the historian.

Shemilt (1980) worked with thirteen- to sixteen-year-olds. He found that children taught through active problem-solving are less inclined to regard 'facts' as certain. He suggested the following pattern of development: evidence as 'information', as giving answers to be unearthed, as presenting problems to work out, and finally as recognition that the context of evidence is necessary to establish historicity.

Although this research is interesting because it shows that it is possible to develop genuine historical thinking, it gives the impression that this is only possible with older children. However, with simpler material and questions, these approaches could be adapted for younger children. It seems important therefore to define, through teachers' experience, based on planning for precise learning outcomes, the historical questions and kinds of evidence appropriate at different ages, and to look, in a much more refined way at children's responses to them.

Shawyer, Booth and Brown (1988) noted that although there has been greater use of sources in the last ten years, there has been little research into children's levels of understanding of the evidence. Three recent small-scale studies have investigated young children's ability to make inferences about evidence; they did not attempt to explore the range of children's thinking in detail, but they do suggest that it is possible to teach strategies which stimulate the building blocks of advanced historical thinking in young children.

Wright (1984) found that classes of seven-year-old children could draw their own conclusions about pottery 'finds' from the past; Davis (1986) asked junior school children to identify 'mystery objects' and found they could make historical statements which were tentative and provisional. Hodgkinson (1986) showed genuine historical objects (e.g. newspapers, candle-holders) and 'fake' historical objects (e.g, mock ship's log), to children of nine and ten years old. He, too, found they used probability words and used 'because' to develop an argument. Marbeau (1988) concluded that in primary school history, we must provide a means for open and animated thought so that the child has intellectual autonomy, can take risks, exchange ideas and organise thoughts relative to the thoughts of others. In this way, a plan or a photograph can come to life.

THEORIES OF COGNITIVE DEVELOPMENT RELEVANT TO HISTORICAL IMAGINATION AND EMPATHY

Confusion over what is meant by empathy in psychology is easily shown. Goldstein and Michels (1985) gave seventeen definitions, and Knight (1989b) refers to many more examples. However, there are three aspects of developmental psychology which seem relevant to the development of historical imagination and empathy: work on 'creative thinking', work on changing perspective, and theories of psychodynamics.

The first area, 'creative thinking', has implications for how children may best be encouraged to make a range of valid suppositions about evidence, (how it was made and used, and what it meant to people at the time).

Since the 1960s, psychologists who were concerned that traditional intelligence tests were too narrow a measure of intellectual ability, have devised creativity tests. Creativity however was also difficult to define. Rogers (1959) saw it as 'growing out of the interaction of the individual and his material'. Guilford (1959) listed traits related to creativity: the ability to see a problem, fertility of ideas, word-fluency, expressional fluency, and fluency of ideas (the ability to produce ideas to fulfil certain requirements such as uses for a brick, in limited time), flexible thinkers who could produce a variety of ideas, or solve unusual problems (which of the following objects could be adapted to make a needle – a radish, fish, shoe, carnation?), and tolerance of ambiguity, a willingness to accept some uncertainty in conclusions.

Guilford devised tests to measure such abilities. Other tests of creativity followed. Torrance (1965) used an 'Ask and Guess' test requiring hypotheses about causes and results related to a picture, and a 'just suppose' test in which an improbable situation in a drawing requires imaginative solutions. Wallach and Kagan (1965) said that creativity can be tested by the number of associates, and the number of unique associates generated in response to given tests, both verbal and visual. Their tests included interpretation of visual patterns and suggesting uses for objects such as a cork or a shoe. Researchers concluded that creativity is a dimension which involves a child's ability to generate unique and plentiful associates in a task-appropriate manner, and in a relatively playful context. Such research has implications for classroom practice. It is generally accepted that the ability to think creatively rather than conform without question is important for individual and social well-being. Teachers can develop divergent thinking both through creative problem-soiving courses (Parnes, 1959), and by creating an environment in which children become confident in their ability to think adventurously (Haddon and Lytton, 1968). On the other hand, Torrance (1962), Wallach and Kagan (1965), and Getzels and Jackson (1962) showed that highly creative children are often not encouraged or recognised by their teachers, who prefer conformity.

The second area of psychologists' work which may shed light on children's ability to understand how people in the past may have felt, thought and behaved is concerned directly with empathy. However, psychologists' definitions of empathy are of limited use when applied to history because they are partial, misleading or irrelevant. Piaget saw it as a cognitive process, thinking rather than feeling from someone else's point of view. His 'Three Mountains' experiment (1956) suggested that young children find this difficult, but others have said that it depends on their involvement, and on their understanding of the situation. J. H. Flavell (1985) suggested that children are capable of making inferences which enable them to see someone else's point of view, but do not see the need to do so. This is endorsed by Martin Hughes' 'Policeman Replication' of the Three Mountains experiment (Donaldson, 1978) and by the 'Sesame Street test' of H. Borke (1978).

Recent research differentiates between visual perspective-taking, conversational role-taking and pictorial representation, and in each instance, young children appear to be underestimated. Cox (1986) said that in their verbal interactions, young children do develop inferences concerning the points of view of others, but more research is needed into the intervening years between early childhood and maturity.

Piaget (1932) suggested the sequence in which children learn about rules: at first they do not understand that rules exist, then they change them according to their own needs. Next they come to accept one set of rules rigidly. Finally they are able to understand that rules change as society changes and are not absolute. In historical terms, they first become able to see life from another standpoint, but only with maturity can they understand that rules and behaviour change with society.

The third area of psychologists' work which has a bearing on how we should develop children's historical imagination is concerned with psychodynamics. Jones' (1968) approach was based on the work of Erikson (1965). He criticised Bruner's emphasis on deductive reasoning, divorced from emotional involvement. Jones thought that children must be encouraged to understand both themselves and the behaviour, feelings and ideas of different societies and that it is essential that cognitive development should be related to emotional and imaginative growth. 'It is necessary that children feel myth as well as understand it' (1968, p. 49). He asked children, for example, to list the kinds of conflicts to be expected in a Netsilik winter camp and how they are solved (through food-sharing, games, taboos and magic), then to categorise their own conflicts and ways of solving them.

Theories relating to historical empathy regard it as both a cognitive and an affective process, although the relationship between these processes and the pattern of their development is unclear. Watts (1972) stressed the constant interaction of deductive reasoning with imaginative thinking in history. The work of some psychologists has shown that the creativity needed to make valid suppositions, and the ability to suggest another person's point of view requires reasoning, but psychodynamic theories show that such reasoning involves an exploration of creative fantasy, an understanding of our own feelings and of how these are part of shared human experience.

RESEARCH INVESTIGATING THE DEVELOPMENT OF HISTORICAL EMPATHY IN CHILDREN

There have been three studies which suggest that in history, children become increasingly able to make suppositions, to understand other points of view and values different from their own.

Blakeway (1983) constructed tasks which she felt made 'human sense' (Donaldson, 1978), were age-appropriate (Borke, 1978), and which made children aware of different perspectives and of the need to communicate them (Knight, 1989c). In the first part of her study, she showed that her class of nine-year-olds could understand the pain and uncertainty of evacuees in the Second World War, and could also understand the thoughts and feelings which might have been experienced by an adult, a fighter pilot. However, the attempt to give the material 'human sense' in that it involved children not long ago, in the same school, meant that the children were more likely to sympathise and identify, than to display an understanding of different attitudes and values. In the second part of her study, she investigated the ability of two classes of eight- and nine-year-olds to make inferences. She asked them, 'What would you have felt if you were the fifteen-year-old King, Richard II, fighting the rebels in the Peasants' Revolt? Would you agree to their demands?' She found that the emotions ascribed to the King were limited to the children's own experience of life. This is not surprising since the difference between feeling fear, jealousy and anger depends on a person's perception of the situation. The older children offered *more* possible interpretations of the King's reasons and three-quarters of them were able to suggest why they might have gone to London, if they had been peasants. Blakeway's study (1983) shows that, by stopping to consider choice, children become aware of the possibilities that are available, they have control over their thinking, and become able to generate a variety of suppositions which lead towards understanding another point of view.

Knight (1989a,b) traced the emergence, in sequence, of four different aspects of children's understanding of people in the past. He tape-recorded 95 children between six and fourteen. He found that the first competency to emerge was the ability to retell a story from the point of view of someone involved in it. Six-year-olds found this difficult, but 67 per cent of the sample could do this by 9.3 years and 80 per cent by 10.3 years old. Next, children became able to explain an apparently strange attitude. They were told the story of General Wolfe, who died after finally capturing Quebec from the French. Then they were asked why he said 'Now I die happy'. Thirty-two per cent of six- and eight-year-olds offered nonsensical explanations, accepting that he was unaware of the dangers and also deterred by them. The older children (67 per cent by 9.4 years, 80 per cent by 12.8 years) accepted that people are driven by reasons and do what seems sensible to them and they also displayed an appreciation of a range of possibilities. The primary school children were not successful on the other two tasks, where they were asked to predict the ending of a story, and to interpret equivocal information about William 1. Knight concluded, like Blakeway, that primary school children have sufficient understanding of people in the past to be worth encouraging, and that they are capable of making a range of valid suppositions. However, both these studies involve understanding accounts and motives of individuals in complex situations. It seems likely that attempts to understand the possible feelings and thoughts of people in the past begin to emerge much earlier.

Attempts to classify levels of historical empathy in adolescents have involved understanding of beliefs and complex social practices, and so have been less encouraging in their findings to primary practitioners. Ashby and Lee (1987) made video recordings of small-group discussions amongst eleven- to fourteen-year-olds, in which no teacher was present, about Anglo-Saxon oath-help and ordeals. At the first level, Anglo-Saxons were seen as simple, and their behaviour as absurd. At the next level, there are stereotyped role descriptions, with no attempt to distinguish between what people now know and think, and what they knew and thought in the past. At the level of every day empathy', there is a genuine attempt to reconstruct a situation and to project themselves into it and a recognition that beliefs, values and goals were different. At the fifth level, there is a clear understanding that people in the past had different points of view, institutions and social practices, and an attempt to understand what a person may have believed, in order to act in a particular way.

Research into young children's thinking in history suggests that, in a limited way, they can make suppositions about how people in the past may have felt and thought. However, this research has been concerned with motives and actions and has not investigated how children may make suppositions about evidence, artefacts, oral evidence, pictures or archaeological sites, in order to understand the thoughts and feelings of the people who made and used them.

PSYCHOLOGISTS' RESEARCH INTO THE DEVELOPMENT OF CONCEPTS

The wide-ranging nature of historical concepts and also the need for children to learn to use the vocabulary of history, has already been discussed (see p. 10). Psychologists have investigated both the sequence in which concept understanding develops and how concepts are learned, and this work has important implications for teachers.

Vygotsky (1962) showed that concepts are learned, not through ready-made definitions, but through trial and error, and experience. Concept development is a deductive process. The stages in which concepts are learned, not surprisingly, therefore correspond to those of Piaget. At the first stage, objects are linked by chance. At the second stage, they are linked by one characteristic, which can change as new information is introduced; children's and adults' words may seem to coincide but the child may be thinking of the concept in a different way; they may have a different understanding of what is meant by, for example, king, palace, peasant or law. At the final stage, a child is able to formulate a rule which establishes a relationship between other concepts and so creates an abstract idea; spears, daggers, guns, missiles are used for *defence* and *attack*; they are *weapons*. Klausmeier and Allen (1978), Klausmeier *et al.* (1979), Ausubel (1963, 1968) and Gagne (1977) endorsed this process and the levels of understanding, with 'concrete' and directly experienced concepts preceding abstract ones, although this is not always the case, or true for all concepts.

Vygotsky suggested that concept development can be promoted by careful use of language. It is particularly significant for teachers of history that he said that concepts which are specially taught because they belong to a particular discipline and are not acquired spontaneously are learned more consciously and completely. The significant use of a new concept promotes intellectual growth. Shif (1935) found that in social studies, when given sentence fragments ending in 'because', more children were able to complete the sentence using a concept consciously learned than using a spontaneous concept related to family situations. They understood 'exploitation' better than 'cousin'. He concluded that this was because the teacher had encouraged them to use 'because' consciously and explained new concepts, supplied information, questioned and corrected, and so these concepts had been learned in the process of instruction in collaboration with an adult.

Klausmeier *et al.* (1979) discussed how concrete, tangible concepts are learned through verbal labelling and through storing images; for example through discussing the characteristics of Tudor houses, the different parts of the timber frame, the wattle, brick, thatch, jetties, pargeting, and by storing images of a range of different examples, language both connects and differentiates the images. As children get older, language becomes more important than visual and tactile perceptions. Abstract concepts are formed by asking a series of questions: What is an axe, a scraper, a flake or an awl used for? Why? How? What is their common purpose? What is a bow, harpoon, spear used for? Why? How? What do they have in common? Then the former are 'tools' and the latter are 'weapons'. Concepts such as 'control' or 'power' involve understanding subordinate abstract concepts; understanding things which give people power (concepts such as tools and weapons), things that have power over people (fear of hunger, illness, natural phenomena), and also the things people might quarrel about.

Research has shown then that concepts are best learned if they are selected and specially taught through illustrations, using visual or tactile examples of concrete concepts, and discussion of abstract concepts. Psychologists have therefore also considered the kinds of material children should be given to discuss and how these discussions may be promoted.

Bruner (1966) postulated three modes of representation in understanding a body of knowledge: 'enactive', depending on physical experience or sensation (a visit to a site maybe or using a tool or other artefact), 'iconic', when the essence of the experience is represented in pictures in the mind's eye (paintings, maps, diagrams, models), and 'symbolic', when concepts are organised in symbols or in language. He saw these three kinds of understanding as complementary rather than rigidly successive. Bruner (1963) said that the questions children are asked about the material must be not too trivial, not too hard, and must lead somewhere, and that we need to know more about the ways in which this can be done. He said that this needs particularly sensitive judgement in history, which is characterised by uncertainty, ambiguity and probability. They must be asked about carefully selected evidence, so that general principles can be inferred from specific instances, connections can be made, and detail can be placed in a structured pattern which is not forgotten. A young child, he said, must be given minimal information, and emphasis on how s/he can go beyond it. Having selected the experience, material and questions carefully, the child must also be shown how to answer them. Learning a particular way of formulating and answering questions may be an essential step towards understanding conceptual ideas.

Little was done to put these principles into practice. Reports (DES, 1978, 1982, 1989) showed that children were seldom taught to present a coherent argument, explore alternative possibilities, and draw conclusions. However, since the invention of the small, portable tape-recorder, there has been considerable research investigating discussion. There is evidence that a tape-recorder encourages 'on-task' behaviour and clear expression of ideas (Barnes and Todd, 1977; Richmond, 1982; Schools Council, 1979).

Piaget argued (1932, 1950) that conflicting viewpoints encourage the ability to consider more than one perspective at a time, and Vygotsky (1962) saw the growth of understanding as a collective process. Rosen and Rosen (1973, p. 32) and Wade (1981) discuss the nature of group conversations with or without the teacher. Indeed, there is evidence that if children are taught the kinds of questions to ask and appropriate ways of answering them, their discussions without the teacher are in many ways more valuable. Biott (1984) found that such discussions were more dense, discursive and reflective. Prisk (1987) found that when the teacher was present in an informal group, children did not use their organisational skills since the teacher was responsible for 80 per cent of the structuring moves. She found that open, unled discussion encouraged children to produce tentative suggestions and to explore ideas, entertain alternative hypotheses, and evaluate each other's contribution. Nevertheless, adult-child interaction is important if it is not used to transmit didactic information, but in order to help children to understand a question and how to answer it.

Current research argues that cognition is intrinsically social. Hamlyn (1982) argued that discussion is necessary, though not sufficient for knowledge: 'To understand that something is true presupposes knowing what is meant by true. 'This involves appreciation of standards of correction and so implies correction by others, and so the context of personal relations. Knowledge is also always a matter of degree in the sense that two people may know 'x' (in 1492 Columbus sailed the ocean blue), but one may know more of why this is significant than the other. They may both know that Charles I was beheaded in 1649 but one may understand more of the reasons why. Doise *et al.* (1975), Doise (1978) and Doise and Mugny (1979) saw cognitive growth as the result of conflict of viewpoint and of interaction at different cognitive levels. Ashby and Lee (1987) found that children reached higher levels of understanding when arguing out a problem amongst themselves than they could achieve on their own, both in class discussion and in small group work, providing they had some strategy for tackling it. So far, there are no sensitive measures for assessing the effect of social interaction on cognition, but Light (1983, p. 85) concludes that we shall see rapid development in our understanding of these issues in the next few years.

There is much evidence however that structured discussion, using learned concepts is essential to the development of historical understanding (despite the findings of the ORACLE survey (1981) and the DES (1983) that very few opportunities were provided in schools for collaborative group work and extended discussion).

Discussion is more important in history than in other subjects because 'evidence', although it may be an artefact or a picture, can only be interpreted through language; it cannot, as in mathematics or science, be physically manipulated to investigate problems. Stones (1979) stressed the importance of teaching concepts, the stages involved, and the strategies for doing so: presenting examples and verbal feedback and encouraging the use of the concept in different situations.

Oliver (1985) concluded that if we are to appreciate the significance of evidence, there must be argument in order to reach conclusions and this must involve abstract concepts, although they will inevitably be rudimentary and incomplete.

RESEARCH APPLYING THEORIES OF CONCEPT DEVELOPMENT TO CHILDREN'S USE OF HISTORICAL CONCEPTS

There have been studies investigating children's understanding of historical concepts: concepts of time, concepts often used in history but not related to a particular period, specifically historical vocabulary, and concepts related to the processes of historical thinking.

Concepts of time

First let us consider research dealing with children's concepts of time. The work of Piaget (1956) suggested that since the concept of time can only be understood in relation to concepts of speed, movement and space, and since understanding this relationship develops slowly, young children cannot understand that time can be measured in equal intervals. Piaget's work on time (1956) is not the most useful to apply to history. He investigated the development of concepts of time in relation to concepts of space, movement and velocity, through scientific experiments. Children were asked, for instance, to draw a succession of pictures showing water pouring from one container, through a spigot, into a container below. He found the first competency to emerge was the ability to match pictures of water in the upper and lower containers and put the pictures in order, showing an understanding of succession and order in time. Next, children understood that the drop in one container and the rise in the other took the same amount of time to occur; they could understand temporal intervals between succeeding temporal points. At the third stage, he found that children could understand that events can occur at the same time and also that temporal intervals can be added together. They then became able to measure time as a temporal unit. Piaget suggested that it was not until this stage had been reached that children could understand 'lived time', 'age' and internal subjective time.

If children cannot understand how long situations may last in relation to each other, or the sequence or coincidence of events, it was therefore often implied that history is not a suitable subject for young children. Peel (1967) concluded that young children cannot understand the nature of history or the significance of time within it. They may understand that William I became King, but not the implications of his reign or the place in historical time into which it fits.

Other researchers have considered the cultural, intellectual and philosophical implications of the concept of time, and asked how central this concept is to historical understanding. Jahoda (1963) said that conceptions of time and history depend on the social and intellectual climate; they are subjective. This approach had been illustrated in a study by Bernot and Blancard (1953). They showed how farm labourers in a French village, whose families had lived there for generations, had a perspective which went beyond their personal experience, whereas immigrant glass-blowers from itinerant families who moved into the village were almost without a sense of the past. People's different perspectives are clearly important in a local study. Children on a new suburban estate, or in an area with a large number of immigrants, will have different perspectives of the past from those in an isolated, long-established rural community.

The concept of time is cultural as well as subjective. The doings of Cromwell, the Act of Union, and the Famine of 1847 may seem more recent to an Irishman than to an Englishman.

Lello wondered whether, since time is not a natural and self-evident order, it really matters that a historical incident should be fixed in context and time. 'Is Herodotus devalued because his chronology is imaginary? Is Thucydides inferior because dates and chronology are almost ignored?' (1980, p.344). Leach (1973) pointed out that the preoccupation of the early Christian authors with a numerical point of view was not in order to record dates, but because of their obsession with number logic. (This is seen, for example, in the representation of time, space and symbolism in The Westminster Pavement in Westminster Abbey.) If this view had not been abandoned, most modern development, especially science, could not have occurred. However, the implication of the change is that time is now inextricably linked with number in Western culture.

Lello concluded that chronology, though of undoubted importance, is not intrinsic to an understanding of time or history.

> Knowledge and a grasp of chronology are by no means synonymous with historical sense. Teaching history involves coming to terms with particular ways of explaining time to children which could, and sometimes does, run the risk of moulding children into preferred patterns of thinking, just as a rigid school time-table segments the day into artificial boxes.
>
> (1980, p. 347)

Friedman (1978) suggested that children of about four years old become aware of time through events specific to themselves and to people in their immediate surroundings; the past and the present are differentiated by words such as 'before' and 'after', 'now' and 'then'. Similarly, Piaget (1952) and Vygotsky (1962) showed how children gradually learn through trial and error to form sets of objects linked by a shared attribute; in the context of history as they make collections of 'now' and 'then', or 'old' and 'new', they try to explain their underlying reasons for the sets they form. Harpin (1976) like Piaget (1928) showed how growing maturity in children's syntax reflects their increasing ability to use conjunctions related to time and to cause and effect instead of 'and'. 'Autumn came and the leaves fell' becomes 'Because Autumn came, the leaves fell'. Harner (1982) showed that understanding these words depended on an understanding of the varied linguistic structures of the past tense and also of adverbs such as 'yesterday', 'before', 'last week' or 'already'. Thornton and Vukelich (1988) found that between four and six years old children began to order their daily routines chronologically from early morning until bed time, while Bradley (1947) had identified a third 'time distinction' beginning at six or seven years old when clock-time skills appear to develop from larger to smaller units (hour to minute to second) while calendar time appears to work in reverse (from days to weeks to months).

Nevertheless, Marbeau (1988) argued that children of six have a very narrow and discontinuous grasp of their own duration and that they build continuity into their existence by reciting it to others and to themselves. Yet he said that this did not impair their interest in the past because they are interested in 'the problem of origins'.

Smith and Tomlinson (1977) studied the understanding of historical duration of children between eight and fifteen. Children were asked to construct two historical intervals from their own knowledge of historical persons and/or events, to make absolute and comparative judgement of their durations, and to provide a rationale for these judgements. First the child was asked to name a historical person or event, then to work backwards or forwards from this anchor point, in one direction at a time, providing a minimum of three items coming 'just before' or 'just after' that in order to define a subjective historical period. The researcher wrote the items on cards. The child was then asked, 'how long do you think that took in history - a very long time, a long time, not very long, a short time, a very short time?'. The same process was repeated with respect to a second historical period, and the child was asked to compare the durations of the two intervals. S/he was asked to arrange the first set of cards in order. The second set was arranged beneath them by the researcher to cover the same distance, and the child was asked, 'Which of the two sets of historical items do you think took longest? How could you tell?'. Analysis revealed a sequence of responses:

(1) arbitrary;
(2) those equating historical intervals with the number of items (well, er, there's more things happened);
(3) those which related the duration to the number of items of a particular type (the longest was the one with the most kings and queens), or to the amount of activity (modern wars are over quicker. Look at the weapons);
(4) a recognition of a need for an independent scale, such as calendar years;
(5) the child is able to overlap synchronous and partially overlapping intervals, and consistently apply an equal interval scale.

The value of such a study is that, having recognised a sequence of development, teachers are able to focus more clearly on the stage of a child's understanding and so to accelerate it. West (1981) found that children have a great deal of information about the past which they have not learned in school, and this enables them to sequence artefacts and pictures quite competently.

Crowther (1982) investigated children's understanding of the dynamics of stability and change. He found that seven-year-olds regard change in terms of direct actions performed and as the substitution of one thing for another, taking little account of the time factor involved, but gradually children see change as part of the universal order of things, of transformation and gradual development, recognising succession and continuity in change, although they show less understanding of the disintegrating effects of change. As one eleven-year-old said, 'Everything alters in different times and different ways. Change can be dramatic; it can come gradually and you hardly notice it at all.'

Complicated concepts of time then involve understanding the language of time, chronological sequences, duration, causes and effects over time, similarities and differences between past and present and the measurement of time. Research suggests the ways in which these understandings develop slowly and piecemeal through relating subjective experiences to different units of measurement of time. Gradually children build up their own maps of the past which constantly change as new information is added. It is a map children carry in their heads rather than a chronological map or a framework of facts.

A current large-scale research project is investigating how children, during key stages 2 and 3, build up these mental maps (Dickinson and Lee, 1994). When the results are available, they will throw interesting light on children's developing understanding of motive (why people in the past may have behaved as they did) and of cause and effect (why things happened). These two strands of the National Curriculum Key Element, Range and Depth of Historical Understanding, may turn out not to be as closely related as is assumed. So far, clusters of ideas are emerging which are, to some extent, hierarchical, about children's ability to explain reasons for behaviour. They were asked to explain reasons for Anglo-Saxon trial by ordeal and for Claudius' invasion of Britain. Responses fell into one of the following categories – children would:

- repeat what happened but not attempt to explain it;
- explain the behaviour in their own terms and so not attempt to understand why it seemed 'stupid';
- think that people were *not* stupid but behaved as they did because 'they were not as clever as us';
- assume that people in the past were very much like people today;
- project themselves into the past in an attempt to understand the behaviour of people who were in a different situation from their own;
- recognise that they needed to change perspective to that of the other person's situation.

An adult, given the same tests, recognised that to understand the motives of people in the past it is necessary to set their behaviour in the wider context of different beliefs, values and material considerations.

The second aspect of the research investigates children's understanding of causes of events in the context of the Roman invasion of Britain, through three tests. In the first, the question is represented as a paradox: there were lots of Britons in Britain; the Roman army was not very big; the Britons were fighting for their homes. So why were the Romans able to take over most of Britain?

In the second test, the children were asked to draw as many arrows as they wished between boxes to assess their understanding of interconnecting factors of different levels of significance and interdependence. In the third test, two brief explanations were offered. One reflected the background to the issue (the Roman Empire was rich and ordered); the other described an event in the process of conquest (the Romans beat the British at the Battle of the Medway). Children were asked, 'How can you have two different explanations of the same thing?'

The findings will be interesting. Such a study illustrates the complexity which underlies an apparently simple statement in the National Curriculum, 'recognise why people did things, why events happened', and the need for research into the ways in which we can help children towards understanding the concepts of causation. This will be the second phase of the project.

Other historical concepts

Other researchers have investigated concepts loosely related to history. Not surprisingly, they traced three broad levels of development. Coltham (1960) chose 'king', 'early man', 'invasion', 'ruler', 'trade' and 'subject'. She asked children between nine and thirteen years old to draw what each concept conveyed to them, to choose the picture they thought conveyed the concept best from six pictures of each concept representing different levels of understanding, to define it verbally, and to choose appropriate doll's clothes to represent the concept. She found that at first, children depended on visual information and personal experience; later they were able to coordinate different points of view with their own experience, and at the highest level they showed awareness that concepts change with time.

Da Silva (1969) gave children a passage in which 'slum' was recorded as a nonsense word and asked them what they thought this nonsense word meant. At the lowest level, he found no attempt to use clues in the text, then a logically constructed response although the meaning changed with the context, and finally a level of deductive conceptualisation, when each piece of evidence was weighed against the others, and a stable definition for the nonsense word was achieved.

Booth (1979) asked secondary school children to group pictures and quotations related to 'Imperialism' and 'Nationalism' and classified their responses as concrete if the groups were based on physical facts in the evidence, such as colour of skin and abstract if they inferred relationships. He found responses were influenced by good teaching, interest and parental involvement. Furth (1980) also postulated landmarks in the development of children's understanding of the social world. He asked children between five and eleven, questions about social roles, money, government and communities. Their answer indicated a growing understanding of these concepts, from seeing society as unrelated individuals, to a grasp of a concrete, systematic framework, at eleven. He showed, for example, that at five, the primary cause for taking on a role is seen as a personal wish, but between five and seven, children stress the notion of order, and by eleven they focus on the idea of succession ('I suppose if someone leaves, someone comes') and the expertise inherent in a role ('Nearly every job you do, there has to be a man in charge'). Similarly, with government, children first had an image of a special man, then of a ruler, then of a job-giver or owner of land, until at nine or ten they understood that a government provides function and services in return for taxes.

Research, then, has shown how concepts develop through a process of generalisation, by storing an image of abstracted characteristics, and of deduction, by drawing from the stored image, adding to it and modifying it. It has indicated a pattern in the development of concepts, suggested that concepts need to be taught, and that they are best learned through discussion.

IMPLICATIONS OF RESEARCH FOR STRUCTURING THE HISTORY CURRICULUM

In the past, primary school history was widely presented as hard facts, not related to source material, described, not explained or analysed. Understanding of different values and beliefs was ignored. There was no clear framework for continuity and progression, which defined the nature of history and its contribution to the school curriculum. There was no method of assessment which was not dependent merely on increased information.

Research, though piecemeal and insufficient, has suggested that young children are capable of genuine historical problem-solving, that they are able to think historically in an increasingly complex way, and that language is an essential element in this process.

There have been a variety of suggestions about how young children may be involved in active learning in history. Palmer and Batho (1981) suggested that children may be taught to select relevant facts from a document, and Cowie (1985) advocated the use of sources 'to provide the slow learner with an opportunity for logical thought'. The Schools Council Project (1975–1980) suggested that children should learn to distinguish between fact and opinion and to see how and why evidence is biased and limited. It said, too, that they should learn to discuss similarities and differences, values and beliefs, in order to infer the feelings and actions of people in the past. The DES (1986) said that children should be shown objects and pictures, and encouraged to ask: What is it? What was it for? Who made it? Why? What difference did it make? What does it tell us about life in the past? Children should then gradually learn not to generalise from false premises, based on inadequate evidence, and that judgements are always provisional and tentative.

Blyth (1982) thought that young children could appreciate how the past was different by looking at, for example, a picture of a seventeenth-century dinner table and comparing it with their own. The Schools Council (1975–1980) suggested that older children may be shown a railway bill and make decisions on the basis of evidence that would have been available at the time.

Egan (Blyth, 1982) said that between four and nine years of age, children are aware of stark opposites of courage and cowardice, security and fear, life and death, and should be fed on classical stories, myth, and legend. The Schools Council (1975-1980) similarly said that between five and eight years, children should learn to differentiate between heroes and villains through stories which illustrate dilemmas and constraints formed through limitations of knowledge, wealth and geographical environment.

Phenix (1964) believed that children learn how values and beliefs change through learning about humanitarian reforms, about moral philosophers, and about laws and customs which describe ideal conditions, such as 'The Bill of Rights'.

However, these ideas for active learning in history are not related to patterns of development traced by cognitive psychologists. Bruner (1963) set out principles for structuring a discipline so that the thinking processes and concepts which lie at the heart of it can be tackled from the beginning, then in an increasingly complex form. He said this required translating the subject into appropriate forms of representation, which place emphasis on doing, and on appropriate imagery or graphics, and that a sequence of complexity in tackling these key questions and concepts must be defined. He said (1966) that this involved leading the learners through a series of statements and restatements that increase their ability to grasp and transfer what they have learned. Problems, he said, must involve the right degree of uncertainty in order to be interesting, and learning should be organised in units, each building on the foundation of the previous one. Finally, we must define the skills children need in order to learn effectively and so move on to extrapolate from particular memorable instances and to transfer the skills learned to other similar problems. This gives confidence and prevents 'mental overload'. Bruner (1963, Ch. 4) believed that 'the more elementary a course and the younger its students, the more serious must be its pedagogical aim of forming the intellectual powers of those whom it serves.' 'We teach a subject not to produce little living libraries, but to consider matters as an historian does, to take part in the process of knowledge . . .' (Bruner, 1966, p. 22).

Bruner was aware, however, that much work was needed to provide detailed knowledge about the structuring of the humanities, and that this has been postponed in the past on the mistaken grounds that it is too difficult. The National Curriculum may be seen as an attempt to structure the thinking processes and concepts which lie at the heart of history in an increasingly complex way.

CHAPTER 3

The Implementation of the Revised National Curriculum for History: A Whole-school Approach

After extensive consultation which revealed concern over a fragmented curriculum, content overload and a complicated assessment framework the National Curriculum for history was revised in 1995 in line with other areas of the curriculum (DFE, 1995). This was designed as a refinement, building on and drawing from previous documentation and experience, not as a new approach. Existing materials produced to support history in the National Curriculum are therefore still relevant. The stated aim was to allow teachers greater opportunity to exercise their professional judgement in planning a balanced coherent curriculum, based on a national framework which would reflect, in creative ways, the individual needs of their own schools.

The structure of the revised curriculum makes clear the expectation that planning should begin with the programme of study for each key stage. A Focus Statement summarises the main ways in which knowledge, understanding and skills should be developed throughout the key stage. This is followed by an outline of the content which forms the basis of study for the key stage and the five key elements or processes of historical enquiry through which the content should be explored. The key elements, which run through each key stage, are concerned with: time and change; understanding why and how interpretations of the past may differ; making inferences and deductions from a variety of sources; organising and communicating results from historical investigations. The ways in which children are expected to respond to those key elements are more complex at each key stage. The programmes of study explicitly recognise that the context of history and the processes of historical enquiry are inseparable.

At key stage 1, the content is specified in the programme of study. Children should learn about famous men, women and events in the history of Britain and other countries. They should learn about changes in their own lives and in the lives of familiar adults and also about a period in Britain beyond living memory. This allows teachers to make choices about the time beyond living memory and the events and people selected. These are value-laden decisions which include, for example, the amount of non-British history taught, and the ways in which women are portrayed.

At key stage 2 there is slightly more detailed specification of content for each of the programmes of study. Life in Tudor Times and Ancient Greece are compulsory, but there are choices to be made about the other four programmes selected. In the first programme of study, either the Romans or the Anglo Saxons or the Vikings should be studied in depth. There is a choice between Victorian Britain and Britain since 1930, and from the six non-European units. The local study over a long or a short period has a variety of possible focuses and may be linked to other units.

Assessment is based on level descriptions which best reflect a child's historical understanding at the end of each year or key stage. They reflect the interacting key elements of historical enquiry which run through each key stage. (Levels 1 to 3 apply to key stage 1 and levels 2 to 5 to key stage 2.) Medium-term planning for a programme of study will therefore inevitably reflect the level descriptions, but these should not be used to plan and assess learning objectives on a day-to-day basis.

AREAS FOR PROFESSIONAL JUDGEMENT: WHOLE-SCHOOL OR KEY STAGE PLANNING

In order to use the framework of the revised National Curriculum as a basis for designing a coherent curriculum which reflects the needs of their own school, teachers need to make judgements about balance, breadth and depth, and about how to provide for and monitor progression. This involves decisions about the structure of the curriculum, the selection of study units and the ways in which these are linked both horizontally to other areas of the curriculum and vertically to each other. Teachers also need to decide the rationale for what is studied in depth and in outline. Issues related to each of these areas will be considered. Diagram 3.1 (p.41) indicates how teachers can sequence the decisions involved in reassessing their long-term planning for history.

The structure of the curriculum

Initial decisions about the relationship between history and the rest of the curriculum are set out in Diagram 3.1(i). Firstly, is history to be taught as a discrete subject or through some history-led topics within an integrated curriculum? Or is history to be linked with just one or two other subjects in a range of different combinations? Alternatively, the curriculum could be structured through themes or 'areas of experience'. In responding to such questions, time-management is an important consideration, so there are strong arguments for integration. The advisory groups were asked to construct a curriculum for history which could be taught in a notional 45 hours a year. Although schools are free to decide how much time should be allocated to different subjects, time remains finite. If overlaps between curriculum areas are not recognised, it seems impossible that children will have time to develop a real interest in and understanding of history, or to pursue their own enquiries and present their findings through a variety of activities. There are also good pedagogical reasons for recognising links between history and other subjects. History is an umbrella discipline; it involves all aspects of the life of a society, its art, music, science, technology, religion. It lies at the core of the humanities and involves children's emotional and social as well as cognitive development. Language and mathematics are systems of communication which are required to be taught in purposeful contexts and a historical investigation is one very suitable such context.

There is also a danger that 'balance' in the curriculum will be interpreted as equilibrium, or distribution equally across all points at all times. A greater problem is that one of the features of the last five years has been the emphasis on the core curriculum and basic skills, with the likelihood that pressures from inspections and league tables will leave the foundation subjects 'positively anorexic'. Ted Wragg (*Times Education Supplement*, 10.2.95, p. 3) used these words when he reminded us of the notorious case in the national press of children in a primary school running riot. Inspectors were sent in. Their conclusion was not that the children needed more basics, but that the basics were hammered to death and the pupils were bored out of their skulls. Some kind of integrated approach seems the best way to prevent history again becoming marginalised and tokenistic. This would be a disaster if children are to develop their own view of the world and of their places in it.

The post-Dearing advice from SCAA (1995) on creating a coherent and balanced curriculum suggests that units of 'continuing work' should be planned across two years in subjects or aspects of the curriculum which require regular and frequent teaching, 'systematic and gradual acquisition, practice and consolidation'. The examples given are mathematics, reading, and personal, social and moral education. History units would be planned as 'blocked work'. Blocked work is drawn from a 'single subject or aspect of the curriculum which can be taught in a specific amount of time not exceeding a term, focuses on a distinct and cohesive body of knowledge, understanding and skills and can be taught alone or has potential for linking with units of work and other subjects. Examples of such combinations given are history linked to geography in a local study at key stage 1 and history linked to English for Years 5 and 6.

This seems a practical basis for whole-school curriculum planning. Nevertheless the integrated curriculum webs from the first edition of this book have been reproduced in Chapter 4 for several reasons. It was never assumed that mathematics taught as part of a topic represents all the mathematics that children are taught at this time, nor that geography related, for example to

Tudor exploration, is not in addition to focused geography topics. Secondly, it is assumed that particular content of mathematics or English will inevitably be adjusted in line with the scheme for those subjects, depending on whether 'Tudors' is studied in Year 3 or Year 6, but aspects of these schemes may well overlap with a history topic at any point in the continuum. Thirdly, although different history study units may be linked with varying combinations of subjects, sometimes with arts, sometimes with music or technology for example, the integrated webs offer ideas about possible combinations; not all links need necessarily be included. However, the integrated webs reflect the principle of curriculum overlaps and integration, and of educating children in a holistic way. This principle is recognised in the SCAA (1995) document as important in developing a coherent curriculum and managing time effectively.

Below are some suggested links between history and other curriculum areas which can be used in planning a history-focused, integrated topic.

I   *Mathematics*
(i)   *Shape and space*
      Properties of two-dimensional shapes:
      identify shapes in buildings: windows, doors, pediments.
      Properties of three-dimensional shapes:
      identify cuboids, cubes (buildings, steps), prisms (roofs),
      cylinders (pillars, chimneys); measure, reduce to scale, make nets and
      models of buildings.
      Maps, journeys, plans of sites.

(ii) *Number/algebra/symmetry*
      Repeating patterns: windows, railings, terraces.
      Tesellations: brickwork, tiles, mosaics, garden design, wallpaper,
      fabric.

(iii) *Measures. Length/distance*
      Measure routes (scale).
      Time, speed and distance calculations.
      Measure buildings.
      Record size (e.g. of ships) by drawing on ground.

      Time
      Time zones, devices for calculating solar time.
      Different ways of measuring time (sand clocks, water clocks, candle
      clocks).
      Different ways of recording time (Chinese, Indian, Arabic, European
      calendars), agricultural calendars, ships' logs, school and factory

time-tables, diaries.
Changing attitudes to and effects of precise measurement of time.

Weight
Recipes, rations, diet. Weight of load carried (e.g. coal carried by child labourer). Weight of cattle and sheep at beginning and end of eighteenth century.
Capacity (e.g. how much beer drunk daily at Hampton Court in reign of Henry VIII).

Money
Price of food, proportion of income.

(iv) *Number calculations and estimations, data collection, presentation and interpretation*
Statistics
Census returns
Street directories
Graveyard studies
Parish records
Population statistics
Trade figures
Questionnaires and surveys

Time-lines
Counting systems in other cultures
Information about journeys can often be found in diaries, letters and oral accounts, advertisements for stage coaches, newspapers and old time-tables. Statistics about trade or population figures can be extracted from books written for adults. Calculations can be used to investigate historical questions.

II   *Language*
(i)   *Speaking and listening*
Discussion of evidence, using selected concepts: (how was it made, how does it work, what does it tell us about the past, is it a reliable source? Supporting points of view with argument).
Interviews and questionnaires.
Listening to fiction about the past, listening to stories, myths, legends, accounts.
Presenting findings as slide shows or on video or oral tape, or directly to audiences of children, parents or other members of the community.

Discussion of how to interpret evidence (e.g. while modelmaking, drawing).

'Home corner' play using old artefacts.

Drama, role-play, debate (did the Ancient Greeks treat women fairly?), improvising stories, puppet plays, 'hot-seating', (what would you do next?), freeze-frames based on a picture (who are you? what are you doing?).

Listening to video or oral tape-recordings.

(ii) *Reading*

Reading visual images (films, books, photographs).

Making books, brochures, posters to present findings (individual, group or class).

Reading stories about the past (consider viewpoints, motives, how true the story may be).

(iii) *Writing*

Note-taking from teacher's presentation: from reference books. Labels to explain what models, drawings, historical sources, tell us about the past (e.g. in a class museum).

Quizzes about evidence (e.g. a museum trail).

Letters (e.g. to museums and galleries or to invite visitors to the school).

Directions (e.g. for other visitors to a site or gallery).

Stories, plays, poems, based on evidence, describing and explaining the past.

Writing presenting a point of view (how true is this diary account?).

Reviews of stories about the past.

Shared writing (e.g. working in groups to write newspapers from different viewpoints).

Writing about science investigations connected with history topic.

III *Science*

(i) *Materials*

Used to make toys, buildings, transport, clothes, tools and machines; what are their properties, where do they come from, how have they changed, why?

(ii) *Processes of life*

Health, hygiene, diet, medicines, now and in the past.

How have they changed? Why? What have been the effects of changes?

(iii) *Genetics and evolution*

Selective growth of crops and breeding of domestic animals; changes in food and farming.

(iv) *Earth and atmosphere*
Influences of climate, rainfall, wind direction, soil-type on settlement.

(v) *Forces*
Tools, machines, transport, buildings.

(vi) *Electricity and information technology*
Effects on daily life (e.g. of domestic appliances).

(vii) *Energy*
Toys; how do they work?
Wind, water, steam, nuclear power; effects on way of life, causes and effects of change.

(viii) *Sound and music*
Musical instruments in the past; how did they work? Music, what did it sound like, who played/listened; when? Song, dance.

(ix) *Light*
Scientific revolution: lenses, telescopes, new ideas about the earth in space.

IV *Art*
Study of contemporary paintings and design.
Observational drawing, developed in other media: painting, printing, embroidery.
Design based on detail in fabric, ceramics, furniture, or in building materials (wood, brick, stone, iron). (Printing, computing.)
Model-making in junk, balsa wood (e.g. timber-frame building), pottery, in order to reconstruct an artefact, building, street or site from available evidence.

V *Technology*
Model-making; making 'props' for role-play or for class museum, or for acting out a story; grinding seeds, making dough, cooking recipes from period; carding, spinning, weaving, dying wool; drawing plans of artefacts, or buildings, using simple machines or tools from the past (e.g. candle snuffer, button hook); copying old designs in fabric, needlework, wallpaper, mosaics, pottery.

VI *Geography*
(i) Making and reading maps.
(ii) Understanding places, reasons for settlement; climate, relief, resources.
(iii) Communication between settlements; social, economic, aesthetic.
(iv) Reasons for changes in settlements or populations.

VII Religious education
 Belief systems, celebration of beliefs (places of worship and festivals),
 effects of beliefs on individuals and communities.

After agreement has been reached about how subjects are to relate to each
other, further questions need to be addressed about the structure of the
curriculum. In what ways and to what extent is teachers' subject expertise to be
developed? To what teaching approaches is the school firmly committed? What
should be the relationship between nursery and reception classes and the key
stage 1 curriculum? How will provision be made for special educational needs?
What is the school policy for information technology across the curriculum?
And what are the implications of these questions for history?

The 1995 Report of the Chief Inspector for Schools suggested that at key stage
2 teachers' subject knowledge and therefore curriculum planning and
assessment is generally still seen to be inadequate. It suggested that pupils at
the top of this key stage might benefit by being taught by more than one
teacher. By contrast, Jim Campbell has suggested that a way forward would be
to use good quality published learning materials so that teachers can feel
confident about the subject content and concentrate on planning how best to
use them (*Times Educational Supplement*, 17.2.95, p. 6). Tim Lomas (1994) gives a
good overview of ways in which a history coordinator can support colleagues
in developing, monitoring and evaluating an effective whole-school history
programme.

Decisions also need to be made about teaching strategies which best promote
genuine independent historical understanding, in view of recent claims which
seem to suggest that direct whole-class teaching involves high level interaction
which does not occur in small collaborative groups. Yet there is some evidence
that there are links between whole-class teaching in history at key stage 2 and
children's ability to transfer the thinking processes learned to small group
discussion of sources when no adult is present (Cooper, 1993).

Another area for consideration is the relationship between nursery and
reception classes and Year 1. There can be a tension here in creating continuity
in whole-school planning between the emphasis on 'areas of learning' set out
in the Rumbold Report (DES, 1991b), and a subject-based curriculum.

How then can this change of emphasis be smoothly effected? For example,
which stories can be told to encourage embryonic historical questions (What
happened next? Why? Why did s/he do it?)? How can illustrations be
discussed, to introduce vocabulary relating to past times (a long time ago,
spinning wheel, turret)? Can collections be made and discussed of old things or
of children's baby clothes or photographs? Such history-related activities can fit
well into a curriculum structured around areas of learning: aesthetic, creative,
human, social, language and literacy, and technology.

Teachers need to consider which key elements and content in each programme of study at each key stage may be taught to children with special educational needs, and how. For with thoughtful planning, history is a very appropriate area through which children can develop life skills set out in Curriculum Guidance 6 (NCC, 1990). It can help them to begin to form impressions about themselves, to describe ideas about roles and about work and to appreciate the nature of change. The past can be explored in many ways through each or any of the senses, through dressing up and play in historical contexts (a pretend old kitchen or a castle for example (Cooper, 1995)), or through watching or being part of a Living History Reconstruction. Some historical sources, artefacts or buildings, can be experienced through touch, and oral and musical sources can also be explored by children with visual impairment. At a time of diminishing resources, special needs provision is not 'cost-neutral'; however, good mainstream practice in history, if thoughtfully planned and resourced, will automatically include provision for a wide range of special educational needs.

History also needs to be planned within the context of the school policy for information technology. This can be used in a variety of historical contexts. At key stage 1, besides wordprocessing, children can use a concept keyboard to find information about a picture or a street in the past or to work out the ages of people in a family from a time-line; they can use a simulation to explore a place or building in the past. At key stage 2, children can prepare information for a data base and search it, interpret statistical information or use a simulation to predict outcomes of a given situation. Videos relevant to history in the National Curriculum are available from such organisations as BBC support services and the British Museum and are often listed in resource booklets for teachers. Children can also use a video camera to record their own reconstructions, interviews and visits to sites.

Selection and sequencing of study units and possible links between them

The choices to be made in selecting study units are set out in Diagram 3.1 (ii). The sequence of study units might be worked out by writing the title of each unit on a card, then arranging the cards on a board divided into three rows of four rectangles representing the 12 terms of Years 3–6 (or four rows of six if some topics are planned for half-a-term's duration). Cards in other colours could be made for geography-led or science-led topics or topics focusing on other curriculum areas. It is then possible to rearrange the sequence of history topics in relation to linked topics in other areas of the curriculum.

Links which could create vertical coherence between history topics and horizontal coherence with other curriculum areas are set out in Diagram 3.1 (iii–vi). When the sequence of history study units has finally been agreed, they could be filled in on the left-hand column of Diagram 3.2 (p.45). As each of the study units is planned in detail (see Chapter 4), the different criteria for reviewing the balance, coherence, breadth and depth of the history curriculum across the key stages could be mapped, using this grid. In the light of the contexts in which the decisions were made, this will inevitably reflect the needs of children in the school, the interest and expertise of staff, local resources and above all the values, perspectives and attitudes which teachers particularly want to promote in their school. As an example, the case studies in Chapter 4 have been mapped in this way.

Small schools which do not have one year group per class can still sequence the curriculum using the format suggested, but over a sequence of years. Years 3–6 can then work on the same study unit but at differentiated levels each year. Alternatively, each class in a larger school could work on the same study unit. This allows teachers to share ideas and expertise, collect resources and support each other, and it emphasises the need to investigate, plan for and monitor progression. On occasions, for example, Years 3–6 could respond to the same source or the same question in order to focus precisely on their different levels of thinking.

Vertical links between several history units can be made in all sorts of ways. For example, a local study might reflect a key economic focus within the community; farming, a port or a key industry such as mining or textiles; there could be a focus on changes in farming or in cloth production through Saxon, Tudor and Victorian times; the changing significance of a port could be traced from a Saxon settlement, through Tudor exploration to Victorian trade in the nineteenth century or a seaside resort in the twentieth. This would encompass changes over a long period of time and also develop economic and industrial awareness.

Alternatively, a focus over several units on images of women might cause children to question assumptions or demand evidence for points of view; this could also be linked to a cross-curricular theme on citizenship. Women are still seriously under-represented in images selected for school books, and when they do show women, the source is rarely interpreted from their point of view (Pounce 1995). The chance of achieving a gender inclusive history depends on the commitment of teachers. Osler (1995) suggests that teachers not only acknowledge great women alongside the men of the past, and encourage children to study the experiences of 'ordinary women'; children should also consider *why* women have been invisible and undervalued. In any key stage 1 or 2 programme of study, children could do this by collecting pictures of women in history books and considering how they are portrayed or by focusing on family life from a woman's perspective. Emphasis could also be put on women as historians in their role as tellers of folk-tales, the guardians of shared memories, concerns and values, within the oral tradition. Anthony

Enahoro has described his own experiences of women as oral historians in West Africa in the 1930s:

> Women were ever our historians. Singing, spinning, now one, then another, now in parts, now in unison, they told of the old days before the coming of white men, of the founding of the clan, of tribal wars, of families, of the great deeds of our forebears, in their small world.

(Hulton, 1989, p. 83)

Similarly, some history units could be linked by an emphasis on non-European perspectives: images, artefacts and stories from other cultures can be explicitly selected at key stage 1. At key stage 2, these can support a consideration of non-European perspectives in the context of any of the study units. However, this requires some effort on the part of teachers because materials were produced so quickly to support the National Curriculum that although they are often technically superb, they do not reflect the changing perspectives of historical scholarship over the past twenty years. Nevertheless, teachers will find excellent pictures reflecting links between Britain and the Americas, Asia, China and Africa in history books produced to support key stage 3 History in the National Curriculum; some of these are referred to in Chapter 4. They can be selected, enlarged, colour-copied, laminated and used in all sorts of flexible ways to illustrate Britain's contacts with other parts of the world, at any period, and to challenge children's perspectives.

Indeed, the revised curriculum offers all sorts of opportunities for creating exciting work in history, as long as teachers can remain buoyant and fly free of the cumbersome clutter which has pinned us down and tended to atrophy our imaginations during the last few years.

However, if history is to continue to evolve as an important and integral dimension of the primary curriculum, it must be planned for in relation to whole-school, long-term development. Schools will need to decide how the policy for history which they have devised is to be usefully documented, in terms of aims, development plans and schemes of work, and how supporting resources, particularly those relating to their own school and locality, are to be collected, organised, used and evaluated. These will include people, artefacts, organisations, workplaces, sites, museums and galleries. They need to decide how the subject knowledge of colleagues, both in process and content, is to be developed and translated into a variety of appropriate classroom activities for children at different levels which will allow them to progress. A range of approaches to informal and formative evaluation which diagnose children's different levels of response will need to be considered, as well as strategies for and frequency of summative assessment, recording and reporting to different audiences. And since curriculum development is essentially dynamic, there need to be methods of monitoring and evaluating the quality of the curriculum, of teaching and learning experiences and of children's levels of achievement. There is further discussion of these matters elsewhere (e.g. Cooper, 1994, 1995), and in Lomas (1994) where the role and responsibilities of a primary school coordinator are set out in detail.

Diagram 3.1

Sequence of decisions	Contexts for decisions
(i) Structure of the curriculum	
• history as a discrete subject	• could provide a continous weekly focus for developing historical thinking, but is notional 45 hours per year sufficent? Can some of 20% extra time be included?
• history-focused topics within an integrated curriculum	• history is an 'umbrella' discipline, involving all aspects of a society; there will be opportunities for English and mathematics with a context and purpose; this will create economic overlaps with other areas
• history combined with one or two other subjects at different times	• flexible, making different combinations as appropriate, e.g. history/art; history/music
• themes based on 'fields of knowledge' rather than subjects	• (e.g. people and their environment). Themes can draw on several forms of knowledge; knowledge and expertise are not necessarily organised around 'subjects'. However, there is a danger of a return to 'rag-bag' topics which do not recognise the distinctive structure, concepts and methods of enquiry central to a discipline
• time allocation (length of blocks, 2 hrs each week, half-term blocks, term blocks, mixture of half-term and term-long topics	• short periods of time may lead to a fragmented curriculum and may prevent children having time to be actively involved in planning and carrrying out their own enquiries, larger blocks may lose momentum; possibly a balance of long and short topics, with longer blocks as children mature
(ii) Selection of periods studied *Key stage 1*: which period beyond living memory? *Key stage 2*:	• Is it best to study a period linked to a key stage 2 topic, or to study e.g. 'castles' because it is *not* a focus in key stage 2?
• Focus on Romans, Saxons or Vikings?	• Are there links with the locality; local resources?
• Victorian Britain since 1930?	• Are there links in the locality, in predominant buildings? Was either period one of significant change in the locality? Is this a reason for choosing related study units (or not)? Is the local study based on this period; is this overlap useful, or not?
• Period for local study	• Key event, building, person, period of growth? are there useful links with another study unit, or is

this an opportunity to cover a different period (e.g. prehistory or Middle Ages)?

- A past non-European Society
  At this stage arrange programmes of study cards on planning grid.

- Links with another programme of study (e.g. Egypt/Greece; Tudors/Aztecs)
  Links with geography topic; links with RE topic.
  Cultural links with local community – or because these do *not* exist?

(iii) Sequence of study units
Key stage 1: child's own experience, and changes within living memory, beyond living memory

Although the programme of study for KS1 says that children should progress from familiar situations to those more distant in time, research and experience suggest that children develop a sense of time *either* by starting with the distant past, which is a stark contrast to their experience, *or* by beginning with their own lives. Can the two approaches co-exist (e.g. a major topic on 'me' plus myths and legends from a distant time and place; a topic on 'castles' plus recent fictional stories about early lives of children)?

Key stage 2: units linked vertically by:
- chronological links

- there is no firm evidence that children develop a concept of chronology or of time through chronologically sequenced topics. It seems more likely that cross-referencing between periods, and devising time-lines of different calibrations is more challenging in structuring mental maps. However, the key element questions relating to time need to be used to develop these mental maps across study units.

- a linking common perspective, or a selection of different perspectives (political, religious, economic, social, cultural, aesthetic, technological, gender), making links or contrasts between units

- a key perspective for several units might be chosen to reflect links with another curriculum area or with a group of subjects (e.g. aesthetic perspective with music, art), a female (or child's) perspective in some study units would redress the imbalance identified in images in available resources

- linking historical question(s)

- an overarching question could run through several units (e.g. why did people move to new lands? What changes were there in people's way of life?)

- a linking concept (e.g. harvest, food, communication, trade, travel, health and medicine
- linking cross-curricular questions (see Buck, 1994)

- this would subsume the theme over a thousand years and allows comparisons over a long period
- this could integrate a cross-curricular theme with a group of study units (e.g. citizenship; in what ways are people different and with what consequences?)

- linking through a focus key

- *either* have one focus key elements running

element or range of focus key elements

through a sequence of study units (e.g. inferences about daily life from domestic artefacts in order to make comparisons between units *or* select a different key element to focus on in successive units to give balance over a key stage

● theme

● the same local industry, port or farming community could be a focus and link with an economic awareness dimension, across a range of study units

Links between content across key stages

KS1/KS2 Myths and legends from an ancient civilisation (KS1) – related non-European unit (KS2); local study (KS1) – local study (KS2); famous person or event (KS1) – related study unit (KS2).
KS2/KS3 local study (KS2) – Britain 1066–1500 (KS3); Tudors (KS2 Year 6) – Britain 1066–1500 (KS3)

(iv) Overlap of history study units
● place for local study

● the local study linked to another history study unit, depending on local resources and most significant period of local history. The link could be through integration or juxaposition

● place for non-European study

● this could be integrated with or juxtaposed to another unit (e.g. Egypt/Greece; Benin/Victorian Britain or Tudors, a past non-European society could be linked with Britain since 1930 and the growth or a multi-cultural society)

(v) Links with other curriclum areas through
● integrated topics

● see links between history and other disciplines (pp.33–36)

● sequential topics
● parallel topics

● e.g. non-European history unit, juxtaposed or parallel with a geography topic (e.g. a locality in Asia/The Indus Valley; Africa/Benin; the Aztecs/Central America)

(vi) Breadth and depth
● In depth and outline content

● The reasons for selecting in depth and outline studies will include: the interests of children and of the teachers; the school's resources, the local resources (galleries, libraries, sites, workplaces, industry), the local ethnic community; decisions made in other curriculum areas

(vii) Assessment and record keeping
summative statements recorded
● end of study unit?

● summative 'best fit' assessments, reflecting the whole spectrum of historical enquiry in a range of contexts will be appropriate at the end of a programme of study if there is only one history-focused topic during the year; this would stagger record-keeping for different curriculum areas over the year. The study unit would need to reflect in depth as well as outline work, and a number of

- end of year?

- end of key stage?

- economical method of record-keeping to serve a number of audiences: teachers, children, parents, governors, inspectors (researchers)

purposes: inform planning, monitor progression, encourage investigative and reflective practice, provide research data

key elements to give a balanced assessment. This would allow children ownership of their work after it had been assessed (e.g. to take it home)
- Assessment at the end of a year across the whole curriculm will be cumbersome, but it could be appropriate if history is taught each week, rather than through history-focused topics.
- This is a statutory requirement, but if there are no intermediate stages of summative assessment, children's progess will not be adequately monitored. (Alternatively, if it has been monitored through a fragmented system of 'tick list' record-keeping without giving evidence, it will be difficult to build up an holistic description of an individual)

A streamlined economical system needs to be devised, through which evidence at different levels of specificity can be accessed by different audiences e.g. teachers' medium term plans for a programme of study with inbuilt assessment opportunities will allow for
- on-going informal feed back to pupils which reflects their individual needs; checklists of work as it is achieved, during unit so that each child does not have to do *all* the planned activities
- adjustment of short-term plans as appropriate
- written comments on each child at end of unit
- selection of samples of work for end of year (pupils can select these)
- end of key stage summative assessment using level discriptions

Diagram 3.2

SEQUENCE OF HISTORY EVENTS	BALANCE			BREADTH						PERSPECTIVES						
	OUTLINE	DEPTH	KEY ELEMENTS	LINKS WITH OTHER SUBJECTS	LINKS WITH CROSS-CURICULAR THEMES	LINKS WITH EUROPE	LINKS BEYOND EUROPE	LINKS WITH WALES, SCOTLAND AND IRELAND	KEY RESOURCES	POLITICAL	ECONOMIC	SOCIAL	CULTURAL	AESTHETIC	TECHNO-LOGICAL	GENDER
UNIT 4 – THE GREEKS			1ab 2abc 3 4 5	Maths Eng. Science Art Geog. Music RE			Med. Asia Africa		Literature Artifacts			Everyday life	Sport, Literature, Maths Language, Music,	Architecture		Women in Ancient Greece
UNIT 2 – TUDOR TIMES			1ab 2abc 3 4 5	Maths (Geog.) Eng. Art Music Science RE		Mary Rose F Armada Sp. F Neth	E and W Indies, Central America, India	Ireland, Scotland (Armada)		Reformation	Trade	Everyday life		Music Art	Timber frame structures	

CHAPTER 4

Case Studies: Plans and Examples of Work

The case studies described in this chapter reflect the planning process required by the revised Order for History. In Diagrams 4.4, 4.7 and 4.10, the activities (what I want the children to do), reflect the outline content in the history study units; this does not have to be taught in equal depth. The aims of the activities (historical thinking; what I want the children to learn) reflect the key elements in the programmes of study. The assessment opportunities implicit in the activities reflect aspects of the level descriptions. Although level descriptions should not be the basis of day-to-day planning, they must be taken into account in planning a study unit if integrated, formative assessment is eventually to be summarised with a 'best fit' level description. However, no single piece of work is expected to be a definitive reflection of the level a child has reached in any strand of a level description, because this needs to be revisited in a range of contexts.

Readers of the first edition of this book will recognise that the original case studies have only been slightly modified to bring them into line with the Revised History Order. This involved a change of emphasis in the planning process. First, activities were considered through which the content and key elements could be linked. Then these were reviewed to ensure that overall they reflected strands of the level descriptions so that differentiation and long-term assessment opportunities were taken into account.

The revised curriculum for history is less prescriptive, allowing teachers to make decisions about what content is taught in detail and in outline and which key elements to focus on in each study unit; single examples of work are not expected to demonstrate that any of the aspects of historical thinking have necessarily been achieved. For these reasons the original case studies turned out to be a closer reflection of the revised curriculum than they are of the original order. This is encouraging because they were carried out before 1991. It was deliberately decided not to replace them because they are evidence that the National Curriculum did not invent new approaches to primary school history, and that all the work that teachers have done in the past few years to extend good practice has not been in vain or irrelevant. It seems unlikely that the present economical framework could have been successfully implemented without going through the pain barrier of trying to make the previous, more detailed document work. However, the Revised Order releases teachers from the straightjacket which many felt had been imposed.

Diagrams 4.1 and 4.2 show plans for local studies at key stages 1 and 2. These are followed by plans for a key stage 1 topic on 'Me', and for key stage 2 Unit 4 Ancient Greece and Unit 2 Life in Tudor Times. Plans for Stuart Times have been omitted as this is no longer a compulsory part of the revised curriculum, although it remains optional and teachers may wish to include it in order to recognise the key issues which run through the Tudor and Stuart periods.

The examples of children's work in some cases reflect their thinking in history; in others they show how the content of history can develop thinking in other curriculum areas.

PLANS FOR A LOCAL STUDY AT KEY STAGE 1 AND AT KEY STAGE 2

Diagrams 4.1 and 4.2 show how a local history study (which could link with local geography) might be developed in increasingly complex ways across key stages 1 and 2 through the sources used, the questions asked of them and the ways in which they are presented. Children at either stage can present their findings to audiences within and beyond the school in all sorts of ways and such presentations can be used as assessment opportunities. Activities in both diagrams reflect all of the key elements which can be structured to reflect a range of levels. Presentations might include slide shows, video and audio tapes, drama and role-play (developed from a home corner reconstruction of an old kitchen, for example), story-telling, a museum exhibition or 'stalls' representing the researches of each group (maybe led by a parent or older visitor). Children can display models and paintings, or make up quizzes and games, use word-processing for impressive collaborative writing or use a simple data base to record answers to their questionnaires. Assessment at key stage 1 will need to be through talking to and observing children engaged in these activities at intervals over the whole project because oral responses will be more detailed, more reflective and reveal more of their thinking strategies than is possible in writing, although labeled drawings and picture stories or stories with 'bubbles' could also be helpful.

Using planning suggestions in Diagram 4.2 as a starting point, one Year 6 class in a suburban school investigated changes in population and settlement in their area; this was greatly influenced by the effects of the railway on a rural community. They began, using maps, census returns and street directories in the local library, to find out when their own houses had been built, who had lived in them and where they had moved from. Then they worked in groups to find out about the three buildings which had been the focus of the previous village community; the church, the farm and the manor house. An initially

Diagram 4.1: *Key Stage 1*

	Starting point (evidence)	Activity
Family	Photographs	Collect photographs of self/family. Put them in sequence/on a time-line. Describe changes, similarities and differences.
	Artefacts	Collect 'old things'. Make a museum. Try to place exhibits in sequence. Explain what they tell us about the past.
	Visit site, museum, gallery: *Site* what happended here. . .? *Museum* what is it for? How is it made/used? *Gallery* clothes, furniture or narrative, in paintings.	*Site:* role-play, models, plans, drawings, stories. *Museum:* drawings, explanations, use/examine artefacts. *Gallery:* role-play, stories about pictures (wear clothes – e.g. Geffrye Museum). Sort and name materials in clothes.
	Oral	Questionnaires, interviews, film and video
Locality	*Buildings* (houses, shops, church, farm, offices, civic buildings) Photographs, paintings, old postcards	Observe changes in structure, materials, purpose: draw, model, photograph. Look for what they tell us about the past, similarities and differences.
	Maps Oral Written sources – old birthday cards, gravestones, birth certificates, family letters	Look for differences, explain. Interviews, questionnaires, stories. What do they tell us?
Story	Family stories Local stories Stories about events in the past Famous people Eyewitness accounts Fiction Myth and legend	Oral Read, discuss, retell, rewrite, draw, act. Books Picture-stories Tapes Film Video Ballads & folk songs Plays Newspapers

Diagram 4.2: *Key stage 2 – a local study*

Sources	Starting points	Activities

Maps
Photos
Pictures
Newspapers
Parish Records
Census returns
Gravestones
Street directions
Local histories
Oral accounts
Buildings
Artefacts
	An important historical issue, linked to national trends involving either:
	(a) an aspect of local history
	e.g. education
	    leisure –
	    (holiday resort)
	    religion
	    hospitals
	    a local industry
	(b) an aspect of local history over a short period of time
		(a) Groups could research different buildings within the theme (e.g. either schools, churches, places connected with leisure), correlating findings on time-lines, through discussion, make display.
		
		(b) Time selected may be chosen for particulary rapid change (e.g. introduction of railway) or because of a particular event (e.g. outbreak of war) or a particular personality.

	(c) an aspect of local history illustrating developments taught in another unit.	(c) Choice of unit illustrated would depend on resources in the locality e.g. a Roman fort or villa, Victorian building, Elizabethan house, or museum or gallery with a relevant collection (a railway, agricultrual, canal, maritime museum).
Cross-referenced to analyse use of different sources, incompleteness, bias, conformatory and non-conformatory evidence.		

recalcitrant group researching the church had, by the end of term, constructed a large pottery model of it, complete with an electronic display board explaining features of historical interest which lit up when the relevant button was pressed. Audio tape dramatisation of related events and music and church lights seen through the stained glass created an impressive *son-et-lumière*! Another group investigated the timber frame farm buildings which have now become the local DIY shop. The third group, peering over the gate of an apparently mock-Tudor detached house not dissimilar to the others in the road, was invited in to discover that it was an Elizabethan manor house, the prototype of the surrounding 1920s housing. This offered excellent opportunities to consider reasons for similarities and differences. Findings were presented in a slide show to friends and neighbours over afternoon tea.

In another school, a local study of a Year 3 class focused on a short period of time, the impact of World War II on the local community, after noticing alterations to a house which a local paper confirmed was bomb damage. After a video-recorded interview with the elderly inhabitants and using a variety of sources, the children worked in groups to attempt to reconstruct life in the house over the decades before, during and after the war. These reconstructions were presented through drama and the popular dances and songs of each decade. The 1950s reconstruction included a Coronation party in which the event was described by talking heads using contemporary newspaper accounts from inside a cardboard box 'television'.

In a third local history study, Brigid Bolton, a Lancaster University student working with Year 6 children, used knowledge they had gained through a study of Victorian Britain (the effects of steam power on the growth of railways, and mining and mass production in northern cities) as a basis for a local study focusing on Victorian Ambleside and the growth of tourism.

'ME' YEARS 1 AND 2 – KEY STAGE 1 LEVELS 1–3

This topic mainly reflects the first of the three areas of study of the key stage 1 history programme, changes in the everyday lives of the children and in the lives of familiar adults. The fourth focus, 'Stories', could be extended to include the other two areas, stories about famous men and women and famous events; this would allow opportunities to discuss why people did things and why events happened, the second of the key elements of enquiry. However, it is not necessary to include all aspects of the programme of study in one topic. A topic in the following year might focus on a period in the distant past, and involve stories about people and events through a theme such as 'castles'.

Years 1 and 2 worked on the theme 'Me' with a history focus. Year 1 concentrated on their own time-lines for six years, which recorded their own experiences of change over time. They brought in their own baby clothes, and

Diagram 4.3: *Core study unit 1. Key stage 1*

Language

Listen to 'oral history' and ask questions.
Describe incidents in own life.
Discuss artefacts, photographs.
Listen to stories, ask questions.

Read pictures, stories, museum labels, birth certificates, shop and street names. Make deductions.

Write questionnaires for parents, explanations for photos/artefacts, stories.

'Me'

A Term's Project with a history focus.

History

1. *Time-lines:* sequencing and describing changes over time, related to personal experiences.
2. *Class museum or house corner reconstruction* How the past was different, from domestic artefacts.
3. Visit to Museum of Childhood: finding out about the past through toys.
4. *Oral history*
5. *Local photographs* Visit identifying and describing change.
6. *Stories:* local myths and legends.

Geography

Identify, observe, talk about photos of familiar places.
Identify activities, *use of* land and buildings in locality.
Recognise adults do different kinds of work.
Understand homes are part of a locality, reasons why people made journeys, different forms of transport.
Describe ways in which people have changed environment.

Art

1. Self portraits.
2. Finger prints – classifying and drawing.
3. Book-making.
4. Designing fabric and wallpapers for dolls' house.
5. Drawing old artefacts.
6. Pottery models of favourite foods/meals.

Maths

Time-line calculations
Mapping positions of dolls furniture

Family trees
Sets of toys old/new, materials, how they work
Probability – in predicting own life events

Science/Technology

4. Oral history — effects of technological changes on people's lives.

3. (b) Sort domestic artefacts: old/new, similarities/differences.

3. (a) *Make dolls' house* with lighting circuit, burglar alarm. Make furniture. Dolls' clothes (materials).

2. Toys old/new. What are they made of? How do they work?

1. *Ourselves.* Keeping food fresh (then and now), Exercise/games (then and now).

R.E.

1. Rules: were they the same/different in the past?
'Moral tales' from old Sunday school prizes, and storybooks today. Rules when granny was little, and now.
2. Places of worship in locality.
3. Myths, legends, stories.

Diagram 4.4 *'Me' history grid*

What I want children to learn	What I want children to do	Assessment opportunities
To communicate awareness and understanding of history in the following ways: (i) sequencing objects and events in order to develop a sense of chronology	Time-lines Make own time-line 0–7 (i) Place photographs of themselves in sequence on time-line (ii) compare with time line for teacher; use words such as then, now	*Level 1* Can sequence photographs, events. Can recognise the distinction between past and present in their lives; in teacher's life: can use language such as now, then, next, before, after. Can use questionnaire to answer questions about their own lives
(ii) using words and phrases relating to the passing of time (iii) finding out about aspects of the past through learning to ask and answer questions which help to identify (a) differences between past and present (b) different ways in which the past is represented using artefacts	(i) bring in 'old things for house corner role-play/class museum Draw them; attach (by Velcro, which allows rearrangement) to a sequence line with categories (very old/old/new). (ii) Visit Museum of Childhood. Handling session – old toys What were they made of? What are they? How did they work?	*Level 1* Beginning to find out about the past from sources of information and to recognise a distinction between past and present *Level 2* Also beginning to identify some of the different ways in which the past is represented, and to answer questions about the past from sources of information through making books or presentation for grandparents, or tape or video recordings for 'Children's TV or radio' can:
Oral sources	(i) write questionnaire for granny, grandad, or older person about life when they were little, or tape-record interview at home (ii) invite several older people who	*Level 1* recognise distinction between past and present, in other people's lives *Level 2* identify some of the different

Diagram 4.4 *Cont*

	were brought up in different parts of the world and in different circumstances to tell children about their early years, to show photographs of themselves in the past and of their treasured possessions.	ways in which the past is represented Level 1 ask and answer questions about photographs which recognise similarities and differences using concepts of time
Photographs	Collect and display selected old photographs of locality; take photographs of /visit same sites today	*Level 2* also demonstrate factual knowledge about events or people beyond living memory, related to photographs
Stories	(i) Invite someone from a local history society to tell 'true stories' about locality which children can retell, draw, act out (ii) Myths and legends from different cultures	*Level 1* can sequence events and use time vocabulary in retelling stories *Level 2* also can begin to explain why people acted as they did, demonstrate factual knowledge learned from 'true stories' and ask and answer questions about the past, based on the stories

Diagram 4.5: *Plan showing how work for the term was organised around four focuses, each several weeks*

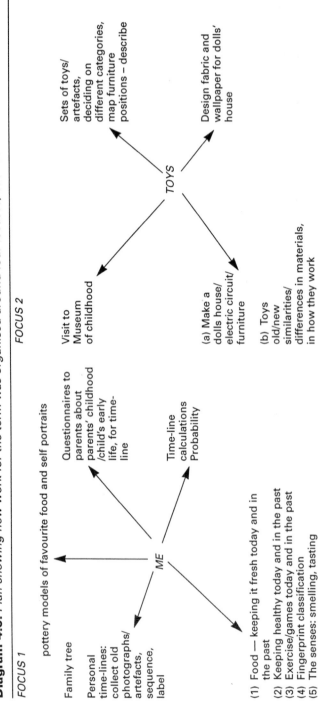

FOCUS 1

pottery models of favourite food and self portraits

Family tree

Personal
time-lines:
collect old
photographs/
artefacts,
sequence,
label

(1) Food — keeping it fresh today and in
    the past
(2) Keeping healthy today and in the past
(3) Exercise/games today and in the past
(4) Fingerprint classification
(5) The senses: smelling, tasting

ME

Questionnaires to
parents about
parents' childhood
/child's early
life, for time-
line

Time-line
calculations
Probability

FOCUS 2

Visit to
Museum
of childhood

(a) Make a
dolls house/
electric circuit/
furniture

(b) Toys
old/new
similarities/
differences in materials,
in how they work

TOYS

Sets of toys/
artefacts,
deciding on
different categories,
map furniture
positions – describe

Design fabric and
wallpaper for dolls'
house

Diagram 4.5: *Cont*

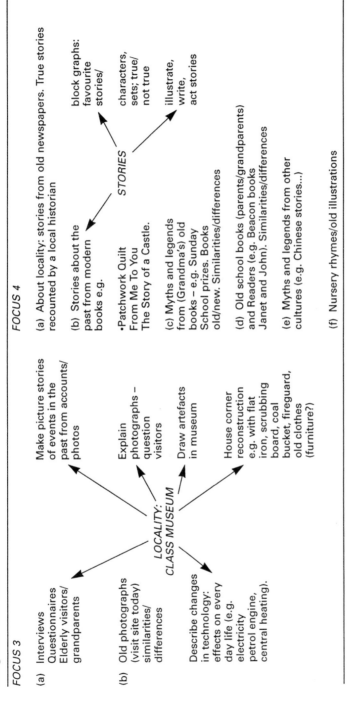

FOCUS 4

(a) About locality: stories from old newspapers. True stories recounted by a local historian

(b) Stories about the past from modern books e.g.

•Patchwork Quilt From Me To You The Story of a Castle.

(c) Myths and legends from (Grandma's) old books – e.g. Sunday School prizes. Books old/new. Similarities/differences

(d) Old school books (parents/grandparents) and Readers (e.g. Beacon books Janet and John). Similarities/differences

(e) Myths and legends from other cultures (e.g. Chinese stories...)

(f) Nursery rhymes/old illustrations

STORIES

block graphs: favourite stories/

characters, sets; true/ not true

illustrate, write, act stories

FOCUS 3

(a) Interviews Questionnaires Elderly visitors/ grandparents

Make picture stories of events in the past from accounts/ photos

(b) Old photographs (visit site today) similarities/ differences

Explain photographs – question visitors

Draw artefacts in museum

LOCALITY: CLASS MUSEUM

Describe changes in technology: effects on every day life (e.g. electricity petrol engine, central heating).

House corner reconstruction e.g. with flat iron, scrubbing board, coal bucket, fireguard, old clothes (furniture?)

toys they had had over the previous five years, sequenced socks and mittens to illustrate growth, sequenced their photographs, and recounted memories. They interviewed one of the parents about a new baby who was brought into school, weighed, measured and compared with them. They listed their achievements since they were babies: talking, throwing and catching balls, and so on. The children were also paired with Year 6 children as part of the Year 6 work on 'human development'. Each pair worked on a cross-curricular theme planned by the older child for a week, at their own level. One pair, for instance, studied an old oil lamp, wrote about it, painted it and found out about it, each in their own way, then they put the resulting work in a book and discussed similarities and differences of the five-year-old ten-year-old approaches. Both the Year 1 and Year 6 children enjoyed this, and it enabled the younger children to predict what they may be like and able to do when they are 'twice as old as now'.

The Year 1 teacher and the head-teacher also participated 'at their own level'. The Year 1 teacher made her own time-line illustrated with photographs of her family and key events in her life, concluding with her Graduation Day and her wedding. Since she was *twenty-five*, this was a *very long* time-line, and allowed the children to discuss their life span in relation to hers, and to compare different scales for recording time. The teacher displayed her own collection of books and toys, surrounding her wedding dress on a stand in the middle of the room and invited her own grandma to come to school! Gran, teacher, and children, all enjoyed exchanging memories. Meanwhile, in the foyer, the headmistress, who was new to the school, took the opportunity both to introduce herself and to support the history project, by making her time-line. This was *very long indeed* because she was nearly fifty years old. She was able to show us photographs of her father leaving home to go to war and other very personal records - a long swathe of her golden hair, cut when she was five, her fifty-year-old teddy, her first mitten. She told us in one assembly, a moving story of how she had found these things hidden in a secret box in her parents home on their death. In other assemblies, she read to us moral tales from her parents' Sunday school prizes. This infant project developed excellent inter-personal understandings and insights throughout the wholeschool community, at far more than ten levels!

The Year 2 extension of the theme was originally going to be 'when ranny was little', but since grannies ranged in age from mid-thirties to about sixty, this was not a very useful title, and certainly did not go back to pre-electricity, and horse-drawn carts. So they stuck to an extended version of 'me'. This was not a multi-cultural school, but a Chinese boy had recently joined the class. He spoke little English and did not adjust easily. The class teacher seized this opportunity to develop his work on 'when Mummy was little' into a rich sub-theme on what it was like to grow up in Shanghai, with the help of the boy's mother. The class went to the Chinese exhibition, and went to see the Chinese

1 When did I first have our first tooth?
   I had my first tooth at five months old
2 When did I first walk?
   I first walked at 9 months

3 When did I first dress our selvs?
   I first dressed at 18 months
4 when did I first read a book?
   When I was 4 years old

5 When did I first draw?
   When I was two years old
6 when did I Start to write?
   I started to write when I was 4 years

7 When did I have money?
   When I was 3 years old.

8 When did I know my numbers?
   I knew my numbers when I was 4 years

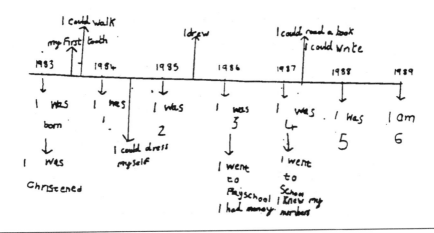

Gemma's family

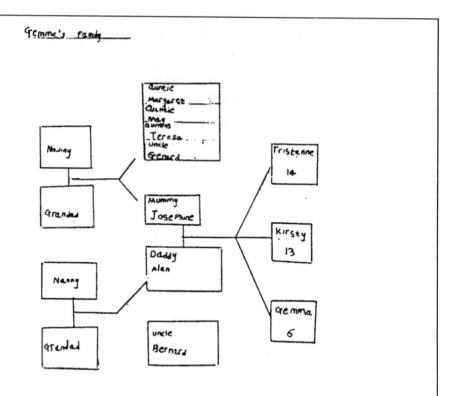

mrs wiltshire dosh't play
with her tds she used nsed
to go tap dancing and she haho
a typewritr her sisters name
was marilyn 1963 she was a
tiny little BaBy she grew
as she got older her nme
was sharon

OUR TRIP TO BETHNAL GREEN
TOY MUSEUM.

On Wednesday, 14th June, we went on the coach to the toy museum.

The coach driver took us to the wrong museum. We had to go on the underground When we got to the toy museum James had a nosebleed.

In the museum we saw old toys: Trains, cars, dolls, games, soldiers, puppets, doll's houses, boats, teddy bears, horses and theatres.

We found out that old toys were made from wood and our new toys are made from plastic. WE found out that dolls were made out of wood, wax, china, clay, paper and plastic. lots of old dolls had real hair.

We had a talk about old toys—it was very interesting.

We were tired when we got home.

A Story by Class 7.

Gemma
Toys

my grandprents would
have pleyed with
hoops and ropes

<u>dolls</u>

Doll were made out of clay
and wax wood and paper and
china and we saw tooth brush
dolls and we saw a plug Face
and we saw Queen Victoria
and the dolls hair was real
and our dolls don t have real
hair and we saw toy town

New Year festivities in Soho. This led to work on old Chinese tales, with big collages and models of dragons and of the 'Willow Pattern Plate', work on Chinese paintings, experiments in writing with a Chinese brush in ink, and Chinese calendars and counting systems. The term concluded with a Chinese meal which Mrs Chan showed the children how to prepare, then they compared old China with what Mrs Chan told them about life in China today, and how life in Shanghai is different from and similar to life in Croydon! The Chinese work gave the project a far richer dimension and also led to greater personal understandings for all those involved. ALO-WA (1990) a book of stories, memories, and photographs written by a black women's oral history group at the Willowbank Urban Studies Centre in Southwark is another example of how rich a starting point family and oral history can be.

Children's work

Some children's questionnaires for their parents ask about the arrival of cats, dogs, goldfish, brothers and sisters, about holidays, cuts and bruises, or moving home. This six-year-old however, is already preoccupied with self-assessment and monitoring her progress!

The information from the questionnaire was transferred to the time-line. There were great opportunities here for transactional writing and for parental involvement. Parental understanding and support is particularly important in family history which can be a sensitive area. The family tree was optional, and done with help at home.

The children were very interested to use the information in their time-lines, photographs and collections of toys to make deductions about the past, and about changes over time. Thes were certainly 'interactive' displays.

The account of the visit to the Museum of Childhood is a piece of shared writing. It refers, in a very sanguine way, to the initial excitement of the day, when the coach driver deposited the children outside Burlington Arcade, telling the teacher, 'It's just up the road love' (assuming they were going to the Museum of Mankind!). Although she had made a preliminary visit, the teacher assumed that this was another entrance. The novelty of the tube journey from Piccadilly Circus to Bethnal Green was so exciting that James had a nosebleed before they were able to discuss such concepts as continuity and change, similarity and difference, during the 'handling session' led by the museum staff. Later, they wrote a book explaining how the toys in the past were sometimes different from theirs, and why.

ANCIENT GREECE YEARS 5–6 – KEY STAGE 2 CORE STUDY UNIT 4

Years 5 and 6 worked together on this project, in a shared 'open plan' area. It began with children deciding to set up a travel agency in a corner of the room, in order to find out what Greece is like today. Eleven-year-olds, boys and girls, often enjoy the excuse for this sort of role-play. They collected brochures, time-tables and posters from local travel agents, made and displayed their own information sheets, booklets and booking forms, and enclosed the corner behind net curtains suspended from the ceiling. They set up a reception area with easy chairs, installed a computer, telephones (unconnected) and coffee-making facilities! Their efficiency compared favourably with the shop in the High Street. Having planned their holidays, everyone made themselves an effective passport (photocopying the front of a passport on to yellow paper and sticking this on to black card, with their school photograph inside) and filled in a booking form. The booking form involved complex calculations of time, speed and distance, money, and also of weight; a collection of possible luggage items was made in a suitcase, ranging from snorkels and sun cream to 'evening wear', which was weighed so that suitable choices within the luggage allowance could be made. Later in the term, one group used the information they had acquired to make a video tape of a 'Travel Programme' about Greece. Groups also took it in turns to cook a Greek lunch once a week, with the help of a parent, and invited a chosen guest. (It was a school tradition to cook a meal on the theme of the class project.)

The travel agency led into the second focus, finding out about changes within Ancient Greek civilisation, by making a time-line, supported by maps, showing key events, people and architecture. The study unit (giving an overview of the period) was introduced through class lessons, describing and explaining the broad historical canvas. This was a useful exercise in note-taking. The notes were then used to make individual time-lines.

The children learned a great deal of mathematics in making their models of Greek temples. This involved choosing a photograph of a particular temple, finding out or estimating its dimensions, reducing these to one hundredth the actual size, then drawing the nets to make the model: a series of cuboids for the steps, cylinders for the pillars, a triangular prism for the roof or portico. They then had to describe their model using listed concepts: angles, edges, faces, height, length, area. This is a useful mathematics assessment exercise because the models varied in complexity, and so did the descriptions, from 'my model has twenty-four right angles' to 'the area of the right angle triangles forming the end faces of the triangle-based prism is 50sq.cm'. Number patterns attributed to Pythagoras were a useful entry into triangle and square numbers and Pythagoras theorem. Learning about and using the Greek counting system was also a good way of testing children's understanding of place value. One child told us that this reminded him of the 'golden rectangle'. Since the teacher was not knowledgeable on this subject, he brought in his book and explained it to everyone!

The third focus was on myths and legends. This was related to music-making in Ancient Greece, a convenient way of integrating the science attainment target on sound, which the whole school had decided to tackle. The British Museum leaflet on Greek musical instruments was an excellent introduction to Ancient Greek stringed and wind instruments, which, we learned, might accompany recited poetry. First, children experimented to discover the variables influencing pitch, then they each designed and constructed an instrument on which a series of four notes of different pitch could be played. This produced an ingenious variety of solutions. They then wrote poems based on stories in the *Odyssey* to be accompanied on their instrument! One group decided to make a tape-recording of a programme for schools explaining how they had done this, before recording their poem.

Another addition to the theme was the news that Derek Walcott, the West

Indian poet, had been awarded the W.H. Smith Literary Award for his poem *Omeros*, which transposes the Homer stories of Hector, Achilles and the fought-over Helen to a fishing community in St Lucia. It also includes a dream-like fantasy of a West Indian wandering in exile in Europe and the story of Philoctetes, a yam-keeper with a 'symbolic wound' inherited from the 'chained ankles of his grandfather'. It cannot be pretended that we read all 325 pages, but the story did offer an unexpected multicultural dimension to Homer, as Walcott puts it, transported, 'across centuries of the sea's parchment atlas'. A PGCE student working in a multicultural school, subsequently achieved some wonderful poetry from Year 6 children with Greek, Turkish and Caribbean backgrounds, after reading them Leon Garfield's version of the Prometheus story in *The God Beneath the Sea*.

The fourth focus was based on a visit to the British Museum. Each group of three or four children chose a particular showcase in Room 69 to study, drawing artefacts and taking notes from labels, in order to find out about different aspects of life in Ancient Greece. In school, they then designed and made an impressive museum, raised on staging blocks, with a facade from floor to ceiling consisting of pillars made from rolls of corrugated card painted grey, supporting a pediment decorated by enlarging photocopies of motifs from a Greek frieze. The exhibits, labelled and explained in the brochure, were mainly drawings of artefacts seen in the British Museum, replica pottery, some modern Greek holiday souvenirs, and large posters made by projecting slides of pictures on Greek vases and copying the image accurately. These were used as evidence exercises, as in 'The Hoplite Race' quoted in the examples of work.

An interesting opportunity occurred for the children to extend the teachers' plans in an unexpectedly successful way, towards the end of term. They had been watching a television programme about archaeology in Greece. Prompted by this, one group asked if they could see what they could find in the rough area of school grounds. Not expecting them to find anything of interest, the teacher suggested they mark off a square metre, and dig for twenty minutes. The results, in an area which had previously been allotments, proved so exciting that a number of other groups ended up undertaking a systematic excavation, which revealed broken pottery, a variety of old bottles (from Victorian to HP Sauce), clay pipes, parts of tools, plumbing, and old shoes. When they unearthed a tractor tyre and the beginning of some steps, they decided 'there may have been a farm house here'. Someone decided to go to the local library for further information; someone else sought out people who had lived in the area for some time, to question them. The children spontaneously decided to make a scale plan of the 'site' where the artefacts had been found. These were carefully measured and drawn, and put on a time-line in estimated sequence, in order to guess what they might tell us about the site before the school was built. The children did most of this in their spare time, no tetanus

Diagram 4.6: *Core study unit 4. Key stage 2 – Ancient Greece*

Maths
(a) *Set up travel agency*
  (i) Plan, book and cost holiday
  (ii) Luggage allowance
  (iii) Route. Journey times
(b) *Make model of chosen Greek temple* (nets, scale, properties of cylinders cuboids, prisms
(c) Pythagoras △ numbers
  □ numbers
  theorem
  golden rectangle
(d) *Olympic Games* (BM notes).
Measuring speed, distance, variables affecting projectiles.
(e) Time-line (scale, measure).

History
(a) *Time-line 1600BC–0* Class lessons, secondary sources to mark 4 periods and key events, people
(b) *The Fall of Troy* Read about excavations and stories from the *Odyssey*
(c) *Visit British Museum* Find out in groups about variety of aspects of Greek life. Draw artefacts and note information Set up class museum and/or make travel brochure explaining what artefacts tell us about Ancient Greece.
(d) *Interpretations.* Pictures from later periods portraying children in Ancient Greece.

English
(a) Stories from *Odyssey*, legends, myths, contemporary accounts.
(b) Debate the role of women in Ancient Greece.
(c) Explanations: science experiments; deductions from evidence.
(d) Travel programme video.
(e) Notes and reference work.
(f) Museum brochure.
(g) Travel agents literature.
(h) Stories – explain constellations then and now.
(i) Poetry writing.

Geography
Set up travel agency.
Make travel programme.
Find out where Greece is and what it is like: maps – towns, relief; climate.
How do people live – food
How do you get there?
How long does it take?

Maps of Europe, Greece, Mediterranean, Asia, in ancient times.

Science/Technology
(a) Sound Pythagoras)
  (i) Find out about Greek musical instruments (IBM teachers' notes)
  (ii) Experiments to discover variables influencing pitch (length, thickness, tautness)
  (iii) Design and make your own instrument which plays 4 notes in sequence
  (iv) Pythagoras' discovery of relationship between length, vibration and pitch.
(b) Volume experiments (Archimedes).
(c) Space. Constellations – (Greek myths). Plot positions of stars on grids.

Music
(a) Write 'music' to accompany your *Odyssey* poem, using own musical symbols.
(b) Play it.
(c) Make tape explaining how to do this for other groups of children.

Art
(a) Drawings from Greek vases (for evidence exercise and museum).
(b) Screen printing – Greek motifs.
(c) Postcards (from 'Greek' holiday).
(d) Posters for Travel Agent.
(e) Wall painting. The Trojan Horse (true or false?).
(f) Greek Museum (+ design and technology).

R.E.
Myths
What questions did people in Ancient Greece ask, and how did they answer them?

Diagram 4.7: *Ancient Greece history grid*

What I want children to learn	What I want children to do	Assessment opportunities
● To place within a chronological framework: events, people and changes in the history Of Ancient Greece 1600BC–0 To use dates and terms relating to the passing of time, including ancient, modern, BC, AD, century, decade and terms which define different periods	(i) Make time-line 1600BC–0 Mark four periods, key events, people, architecture 1600–1150BC Mycenean 1000–479BC Expansion 478–405BC Golden Age 336–30BC Hellenistic (ii) Find out about each period. Write notes e.g. Mycenean metal work Mycenean beehive tombs Mycenean writings; fall of Mycenae	*Level 3* Can make sets of 'Ancient Greek' and 'not Ancient Greek'. Can describe to an audience changes indicated by the time-line, using some dates and special vocabulary. Can explain a key event, for example, why as one of Xerxes' soldiers you were defeated
	Greek emigration to Asia Minor, Black Sea, Africa, trade city states, farming, Persian wars and victory of Athens	
● To learn about the characteristic features of each period from reference books containing photographs of artefacts, buildings, sites	Greek temples, Athenian democracy, theatres, Socrates, war between Athens and Sparta	*Level 4* Can describe different features of one of these periods (in groups) from information collected
● To describe changes explain reasons for and results of situations make links between main changes and events	Alexander the Great – Empire in N. Africa and Asia Greek medicine, mathematics and science Olympic Games, theatre	*Level 5* Can identify 'military' events (fall of Mycaenae, defeat of Persia, defeat of Athens, Alexander's Empire) and say how they caused other changes described by time-line
	(iii) draw maps to illustrate changes,	*Level 3* Can offer archaeological and

To identify and give reasons for different ways in which the past is represented and interpreted	making significant places, dates, routes (i) from secondary sources find out about archaeological excavations around possible sites of Troy (ii) read stories from the Trojan Wars (*Iliad*) and stories about the journey of Odysseus (*Odyssey*)	legendary information about Troy
	(iii) 'Dig' in waste area of school grounds Draw a diagram of site and measure in square metres Collect 'finds' Draw and record plan where found	*Level 4* Can write archeologist's reports saying what artefact found in the school 'dig' tells us for certain about the past, what reasonable guesses can be made about it and what cannot be known
	(iv) Read stories about journey of Odysseus	*Level 5* The story of the Trojan Horse, true or false? Divide paper into two columns and list factual and legendary evidence
To find out about Ancient Greece from: reference books	Visits to British Museum (Room 69)	*Level 3* Can write explanatory label for artefact drawn in British Museum (or for musical instrument, model temple or Greek vase painting)
artefacts in British Museum (Room 69)		*Level 4* Can write a brochure for museum or for tourists to Greece, using variety of sources
resources related to British Museum visit (slides, postcards, information sheets on musical instruments, textiles, lives of women, Olympic Games)		*Level 5* Can group sources used in brochure or presentation and explain usefulness in investigating a particular aspect of everyday life.
To describe and explain to others orally and in writing, individually and in	Display drawings (and postcards and clay models) in a 'class museum'	

groups, the products of their investigations related to:

time-lines

. models of Greek temples

. 'Greek' musical instruments to accompany stories from the *Odyssey*, tape-recorded

. brochures and posters made for the travel agency

. inferences made from Greek vase paintings which are explored in a variety of artistic media

. museum of Ancient Greece

. display and explanation of 'finds' in 'school dig'

Write labels explaining what they tell us about life in Ancient Greece

Take visitors on guided tour of 'museums' or other classroom displays and explain significance

To be able to discuss, as a result of these investigations, the links between Ancient Greece and the modern world (e.g. in literature, language, mathematics, architecture, art, politics, sport).

68

Diagram 4.8: *Plan showing how work for the term was organised around four focuses*

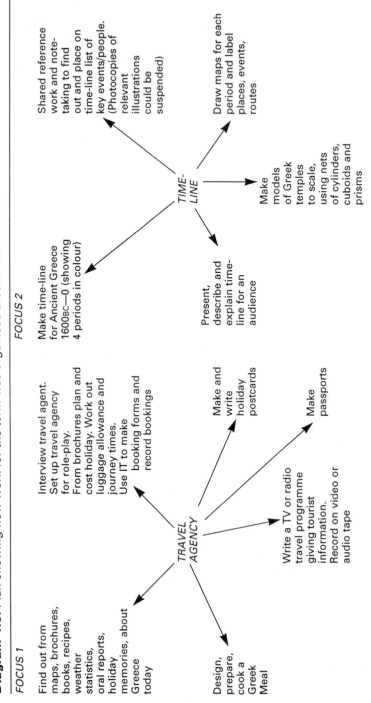

FOCUS 1

Find out from maps, brochures, books, recipes, weather statistics, oral reports, holiday memories, about Greece today

Interview travel agent. Set up travel agency for role-play. From brochures plan and cost holiday. Work out luggage allowance and journey times. Use IT to make booking forms and record bookings

Make and write holiday postcards

Make passports

Write a TV or radio travel programme giving tourist information. Record on video or audio tape

Design, prepare, cook a Greek Meal

TRAVEL AGENCY

FOCUS 2

Make time-line for Ancient Greece 1600BC—0 (showing 4 periods in colour)

Present, describe and explain time-line for an audience

TIME-LINE

Shared reference work and note-taking to find out and place on time-line list of key events/people. (Photocopies of relevant illustrations could be suspended)

Draw maps for each period and label places, events, routes

Make models of Greek temples to scale, using nets of cylinders, cuboids and prisms

Diagram 4.8: *Cont*

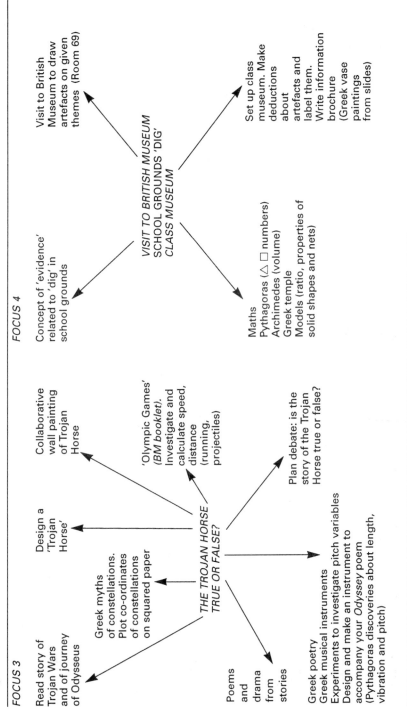

FOCUS 3

Read story of
Trojan Wars
and of journey
of Odysseus

Design a
'Trojan
Horse'

Collaborative
wall painting
of Trojan
Horse

Greek myths
of constellations.
Plot co-ordinates
of constellations
on squared paper

'Olympic Games'
(*BM booklet*).
Investigate and
calculate speed,
distance
(running,
projectiles)

*THE TROJAN HORSE
TRUE OR FALSE?*

Plan debate: is the
story of the Trojan
Horse true or false?

Poems
and
drama
from
stories

Greek poetry
Greek musical instruments
Experiments to investigate pitch variables
Design and make an instrument to
accompany your *Odyssey* poem
(Pythagoras discoveries about length,
vibration and pitch)

FOCUS 4

*VISIT TO BRITISH MUSEUM
SCHOOL GROUNDS 'DIG'
CLASS MUSEUM*

Visit to British
Museum to draw
artefacts on given
themes (Room 69)

Concept of 'evidence'
related to 'dig' in
school grounds

Set up class
museum. Make
deductions
about
artefacts and
label them.
Write information
brochure
(Greek vase
paintings
from slides)

Maths
Pythagoras ($\triangle$ $\square$ numbers)
Archimedes (volume)
Greek temple
Models (ratio, properties of
solid shapes and nets)

BOOKING FORM

Travellers Katie Snowden, Susan Hailstones

Destination Cyprus Paphos

Accomodation The Annabelle four star hotel

Transport British airways 757

Distance 3600 km

Departure time 17.45

Arrival time 23.59

Duration of Journey 6 hr 14 mins - 2 hr = 4 hr 14 mins

Speed 580 K.ph

Date of departure Monday 11th June

Luggage weight luggage allowance 20 Kgs

Cost per person £769 + £322 + £217 + £248

Car Hire Metro = 1550 × 14 = 217

Insurance £75

---

jabs were required, and it proved an excellent way of evaluating the historical thinking processes they had learned and were able to transfer.

Finally, it seems important to stress that neither of the teachers had any specialist knowledge of Ancient Greece, and since the project took place in the Spring term after a very short Christmas break, they had little preparation time. Their own initial reading was limited to a selection of children's books from the local library, and to *The Times Atlas of Ancient Civilizations* (1989). It is salutary that teachers do not need to feel inadequate if they do not have specialist knowledge of a period as long as they are prepared to share the excitement of the learning process. This is probably of greater educational value. (However, we were told that 'The Golden Age of Greece' is a Victorian idea, no longer held by historians!)

> ### The Hoplite Race
>
> On our wall we have a painting of a Greekvase. The picture on the vase shows 'The Hoplite Race', one of the races in the Greek Olympic games.
>
> ### What We Know For Certain
>
> They Caried their shields ∴ they were very strong. They raced naked and did not wear any shoes. They wore their helmits and their shields were half as big as they were. Two shields are the same so they were on the same side. They were men
>
> ### What Reasnable Guesses can we make
>
> It might have been at the begining of the race because the runners are close together. It might be a race with just 4 people because there is 4 people on our picture. It might have been a relay because they might use theie shields for batons. It might be a training sesion. Maybee they did not really wear their helmits and Caried. Carry their shields. Maybee

Children's work

Filling in the holiday booking form designed by the travel agency involved collaborative calculations: reading time-tables, the twentyfour hour clock, understanding time zones, ratio and distances, reading calendars, weight and money calculations involving large numbers, approximation, and the four rules of number.

Large, carefully observed white on black paintings taken from projected slides of pictures on Greek vases decorated the class museum and were a basis for discussion of what they might tell us about Ancient Greece.

The British Museum booklet on the role of women in Ancient Greece, which

> The bloke who did the painting put them in to show they were knights. Perhaps they carried these shields to test their strength.
>
> <u>What I would like to know.</u>
>
> I would like to know why did they not wear any clothes? Was it a relay? Why did they have their weapons? How tall and how old were the athletes? Were they married? Why was it painted in black and white?

contained quotations from contemporary male and female writers, seemed a good subject for discussion. This child's writing, however, shows how difficult it is to make a distinction between attitudes and values today and in the past, and the reasons why they may be different. Maybe the issue was too complex or the discussion not sufficiently structured by the teacher. Nevertheless, there is an incipient understanding that life in Ancient Greece was different. The child has applied her knowledge from another source that women had no political voice, then used this as a yard stick against society today, both in Britain and in other places. Although the ideas seem incoherent, there is evidence of reasoning, of recognising that the past was different, and yet some issues remain similar.

The huge mural of the Trojan Horse which the children painted dominated the 'book corner' and was a suitable background for reading Greek myths and legends. The children attempted to make a distinction between what was probably true and what was legend. This example shows that it is not difficult to suggest what is 'false' supported by a reason, because . . . , or but . . . True aspects are more difficult to define or justify, because both supporting evidence and the child's knowledge of it is very limited.

A British Museum pamphlet introduced work on Greek musical instruments. This was followed by a science investigation to discover the variables influencing pitch. Children then designed and made their own 'instruments', which would play a sequence of four notes of different pitch. There was a rich variety of designs involving pipes or rubber bands. These were used to accompany poems based on the Odyssey stories. The Whirlpool was one such poem. Music was written using non-standard symbols. The description of the Golden Rectangle was discovered in a book at home by a child who demonstrated it in school for the benefit of the class and the teacher.

Odyssey, True or False?

True	False.
I think there was a prinsess that was captured but I am not so.shure. shore (sure) that she was called Helen.	I do not think that there was a wooden horse because how could they have made it so big in a day.
I think there was a battle but I don't.know. think it hapened like the Odyssey says.	I do not belive a word of the Cyclops story for I do not believe in giants.
I think there was a woman called Circe.	I do not believe that Circe turned the men .it. into pigs but she might have cast a spell on them
I believe the syrans exsisted and sang thier songs.	I do not think that scylla the six headed mostr exsisted but I do think there was a whirlpool.
I think that Ulysses wife was called penelope.	

My thoughts

I disagree about women are wretched
and har to be their husbands 'slave.
Why cap'n t women go were ewhere they
like with out asb asking ther husbands.
Most women in the UK don't go to work
but stay home to clean and look after
children Most of the men in the UK
oovn only see there children in
the early morning and late evening.

Then again in anient Greece peoaple
might think diffrently because the
whole world was diftrent then. The
anicent Greeks propaly had no say
in the matter which is a big problem
in todays parliament. There are still
only a few women in parliament. But
in ancient Greece women never voted.
There are still place's in the world were
this is true.

Surely, of all creatures that have life and will, we women
Are the most wretched. When for an extravagant sum,
We have bought a husband, we must then accept him as
Possessor of our body. This is to aggravate
Wrong with worse wrong. Then the great question:
  will the man
We get be bad or good? For women, divorce is not
Respectable; to repel the man, not possible

Euripides, Medea

Science investigation. - Sound.

What we wanted to find out.

We wanted to find out how we could change the note of a string.

What we did.

First we put an elastic band round a cup a plucked it, to make a sound. First we changed the thickness of the band. The thicker band made a lower sound. Then we changed the tightness of the band. The Tighter band made a higher sound. Then we Put a pencil under the ×cub× cup. The pencil changed the sound to a lower sound.

Conclusion.

We found out that you could change the note of a band by a) Thickening the band b) Change the tightness of the band c) putting ×an× a pencil under the cup.

How we made a string Instrument.

Task.

What we had to do was to make a string Instrument with notes tuned to a musical scale. [1]

of different pitch.

What we did.

First we got a piece of wood and we banged 3 nails in. (A, B and C.) Then we got 'string J' and tied one end to 'nail A'. We then banged in nails D and G and wound string J round nail D and fastened it to nail G. We then did the same with the other 2 strings (K and L) and it finished off like this:

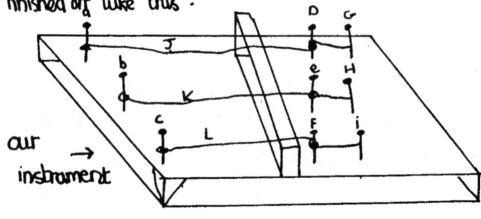

our → instrument

The Whirlpool.

Verse 1.

Between two rocks, near Syran island.
lies the whirlpool,
Water twisting.
Swirling, whirling, foam unfurling.
Sucking ships into its vortex.

Verse 2.

Six headed Scylla hungrily waits,
In her cave,
Suddenly moving;
Swirling, whirling, foam unfurling.
Swallowing men on passing ships.

Verse 3.

Ulysses ship sailed near the rocks,
survived the whirlpool,
faced the monster.
Swirling, whirling, foam unfurling,
Scylla ate 6 men - then safety.

The Golden Rectangle.

The construction of a Golden Rectangle begins with a square (shaded). Which is divided into two parts, by the line E to F. This (Point F) is the centre of a circle whose radius is the diagonal line F to C. An arc of the circle is drawn (C to G) and the base line (A to D) is extended to join with it. This becomes the base of the rectangle. The new side (H to G) is now drawn at right angles to the new base, and the line is brought out to meet it. The ratio between the sides in a golden rectangle is 1 : 1·6. The golden rectangle is a satisfying shape for a building.

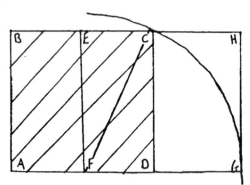

LIFE IN TUDOR TIMES, STUDY UNIT 2, YEARS 5 AND 6

The unit on Life in Tudor Times began with an initial overview of the period; Henry VIII and the break with Rome, followed by rivalry with Spain over religion and trade in the 'New World' which led to the Armada of 1588. Key events were located on a class time-line. Two focuses were selected within this topic, one on 'Houses' and one on 'Ships'. These focuses were chosen because they allowed children to explore aspects of Tudor history which represent complex underlying changes, in ways which they could understand. 'Houses' included both a visit to Hampton Court, the showpiece of Henry VIII's new

Diagram 4.9: *Core study unit 2. Key stage 2 – Tudor times (Part one)*

History

(i) Time-line 1485-1603

(ii) Tudor Houses
(a) Visit to Hampton Court: interpreting evidence — chapel cushions, kitchen, chimneys, astronomical clock, tapestries, drains.
(b) Timber-frame buildings. Use inventory to furnish your house.

(iii) Tudor ships
(a) Visit to Mary Rose. Interpreting evidence, weapons, clothes, leisure.
(b) The Armada.

(iv) Reconstructions.

Maths

(i) Estimate size of a particular house, measure, draw nets to scale, construct, fill in sheet on concepts learned: (measures, ratio, shape and space).
(ii) Voyages of exploration: time and distance calculations.
(iii) Data presentation – Tudor sailors' diet.

Science

(i) Testing roof truss designs. Designing and making a timber frame barn in balsa wood.

(ii) Astronomical clock (earth in space...).

(iii) Mass
Density } why did the Mary
Gravity } Rose sink?
Experiments.

R.E.

The Reformation.
Different ways of worshipping God – now and then.
Conscience: Thomas More and Elizabethan martyrs.
Politics and religion.

Geography

(1) Trade routes to India and East Indies (spices, gold, silver, silk), to West Indies (sugar cane, silver, gold. Competition and piracy with Spain. Descriptions of relations with local communities from points of view of indigenous Indians, Spanish, British, and West Africans.

(2) Akbar the Great. Mughal miniatures: garden, dress, buildings – cultural influences on Elizabethan England.

English

(i) Class novel: 'A Traveller in Time' - A. Uttley.
(ii) Discussion of evidence....
(iii) Armada Day. Collect information about Armada from Spanish, Scots, English Protestants, English RCs). In groups, write broadsheet from your point of view. Write it and produce using IT (front page). Evaluate your group and paper. Compare with newspaper accounts from different viewpoints today.

Art

(i) Design book covers based on 'Elizabethan Embroidery' Victoria and Albert Museum. HMSO (1968). or on lino-print of political cartoon.

(ii) Drawings at Hampton Court and Mary Rose for class museum.

(iii) Portraits of Henry VIII, of Elizabeth I. What do they tell us? How valid are they as evidence?

Music

Tallis and Arne.
Listen to tapes.
Play on recorders.
Make up Tudor dances.

Diagram 4.10: *Study unit 2: Life in Tudor Times*

What I want children to learn: key elements	What I want children to do	Assessment opportunities: level descriptions
● To place events, people, changes within a chronological framework ● To use dates and terms relating to the passing of time (e.g. century, decade, Tudor, Elizabethan, court, monarch, civilisations, trade) To explain to others: Reasons for and results of events, situations, changes and to make links between events and situations	(i) Make a class time-line 1485–1603, put on key events learned through class lessons and reference work (e.g. related to Reformation, voyages of exploration, Armada, Monarchs)	*Level 3* Give a presentation to an audience, explaining the time-line with some explanation of causes and effects of events shown (e.g. of Reformation or of Drake's voyages to central America, or of Armada) *Level 4* Can use more factual information and more detailed explanations to play a 'chaining game' which involves (orally or through devising clue cards) thinking of all possible effects of an event
● To select, organise and communicate historical information ● To identify characteristic features of the Tudor period: buildings, clothes, music, drama	(ii) In groups, use variety of resource materials to collect pictures and other information and make a book (or display) on one of the following, in Tudor times: homes of different kinds; work; leisure (including theatres and music); health; trade	*Level 5* Can devise a game involving selecting 'cause' or 'consequence' cards for a situation and explain what links there are between them (scoring based on number of reasonable causes/consequences identified) *Level 4* Can explain overarching and characteristic features of one of the group books
● Have some understanding of diversity of political and religious ideas, beliefs and attitudes of men and women in Tudor times ● Describe and identify reasons for and results of Armada	Collect information about the Armada ('press releases' can be pre-selected by teacher) In groups (English, Protestants, English Catholics, Dutch, Scottish, Spanish, French) write a broadsheet account from	*Level 3* Can show a restricted perspective in broadsheet article *Level 4* Can try to explain a given perspective in a broadsheet article

Diagram 4.10: *Cont*

● Give reasons for different ways in which the past is represented and interpreted ● Have some understanding of the reasons for the symbolism of and attitudes and values represented in portraits of Henry VIII and of Elizabeth I	one of these perspectives Look at postcards of portraits from National Gallery of (a) Henry VIII (b) Elizabeth I (i) Discuss to what extent they tell what the person was really like, and what else (symbolism) they represent (ii) Compare with written sources describing Henry VIII and Elizabeth I (given on p.00)	*Level 5* Can suggest reasons why events and personalities in broadsheets are portrayed differently Level 3 Can explain why the portraits are idealised images *Level 4* Can describe differences between written sources and portrait *Level 5* Can explain why portraits and written sources tell different story?
1. Ask questions and make deductions and inferences about life in Tudor Times from a variety of sources (a) at Hampton Court: e.g. tennis court (leisure) chapel (beliefs) furniture, kitchens, cellars (food, daily life) paintings, images of Henry VIII; the Field of the Cloth of Gold astronomical clock (understanding of time and space) (b) in Mary Rose Museum: e.g. the ship and its contents (clothes, tools, leisure, weapons, medicine) 2. Organise findings, record and communicate audience	1. Visit Hampton Court. Drawings and photographs used in school as clues to find out what they may tell us about Henry VIII and his court 2. Visit Mary Rose and Museum, Portsmouth. Use drawings and photographs as clues to find out about life on board a Tudor ship. Present information in poster or book or as a video or audio tape for an audience	*Level 3* Can make inferences from selected sources; and write explanatory label *Level 4* Can combine inferences from several sources to write a poster, possibly using one piece of evidence to answer a question raised by another, e.g. how was the gun (on Mary Rose) fired?; use dates and special vocabulary where appropriate (e.g. court, monarch) *Level 5* Can select and evaluate sources using them in a structured way to make a book or a video investigating a historical question (e.g. who were the people on board the Mary Rose? Why did the Mary Rose sink?

82

Diagram 4.11: *Plan showing how work for the term was organised around three focuses*

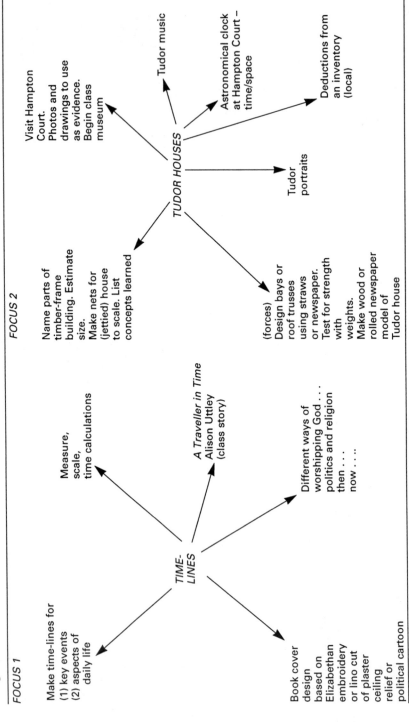

FOCUS 1

FOCUS 2

TIME-LINES

Make time-lines for
(1) key events
(2) aspects of
daily life

Measure,
scale,
time calculations

A Traveller in Time
Alison Uttley
(class story)

Different ways of
worshipping God . . .
politics and religion
then . . . .
now . . . .

Book cover
design
based on
Elizabethan
embroidery
or lino cut
of plaster
ceiling
relief or
political cartoon

Name parts of
timber-frame
building. Estimate
size.
Make nets for
(jettied) house
to scale. List
concepts learned

(forces)
Design bays or
roof trusses
using straws
or newspaper.
Test for strength
with
weights.
Make wood or
rolled newspaper
model of
Tudor house

TUDOR HOUSES

Visit Hampton
Court.
Photos and
drawings to use
as evidence.
Begin class
museum

Tudor music

Astronomical clock
at Hampton Court –
time/space

Deductions from
an inventory
(local)

Tudor
portraits

Diagram 4.11: *Cont*

FOCUS 3

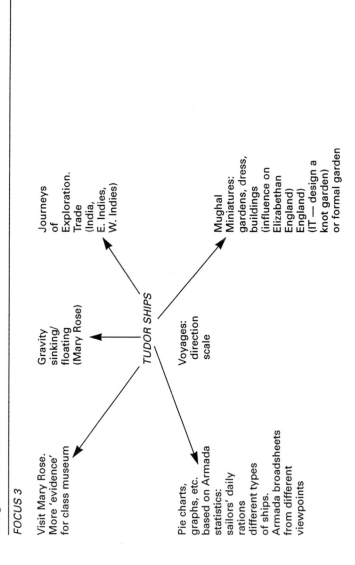

Visit Mary Rose.
More 'evidence'
for class museum

Gravity
sinking/
floating
(Mary Rose)

Journeys
of
Exploration.
Trade
(India,
E. Indies,
W. Indies)

TUDOR SHIPS

Voyages:
direction
scale

Mughal
Miniatures:
gardens, dress,
buildings
(influence on
Elizabethan
England)
England)
(IT — design a
knot garden)
or formal garden

Pie charts,
graphs, etc.
based on Armada
statistics:
sailors' daily
rations
different types
of ships.
Armada broadsheets
from different
viewpoints

LA GRENOUILLE

"

10/7/1588

STAY OR DIE

The Duke of Madina Sidonia commented that if any Spanish Captain fails to maintain his position the penalty would be death, by hanging.
Soon the English are expected to run out of ammunition and surrender to the Spanish and the noble king Phillip II is once more going to demonstrate his enormous power. We are all behind him in the forthcoming final few battles at the sea.

THE PRIESTHOLE   1d

11 AUGUST 1588

SAIL AWAY, SAIL AWAY, SAIL AWAY

9 July 1588 6.0pm Captain Fleming of the Golden Hind has sigalled the sighting of the Spanish fleet off the Lizard.
The tide will not allow the English fleet at Plymouth under Admiral Lord Howard of Effingham to put to sea till 9.0pm.
4 vessels of the English fleet managed to use their boats and anchors to warp out of Plymouth harbour before 9.0pm.
July 30 3.0pm Armada sighted by the English fleet to the south of Eddystone Lighthouse.
Beacons are reported to have been lit from Cornwall to London, local militia being organised to defend the English coastline.
July 31st the English pinnace Disdain opened fire off Plymouth at the rata encoranada.
At 9.0am this morning the Spanish flagship raised her national flag to signal the beginnning.
After a four hour battlethe Armada continues eastwood with the English in pursuit. Medina Sadonya gives the order for the fleet to form a cresant with the more heavily armed ships positioned at the horns. Drake reportedto have left fleet during the night to investigate sails to the south.

style of government and also to a nearby timber-frame Elizabethan house representing the increasing wealth of the new 'gentry'. 'Ships' began with a visit to the Mary Rose, which represented the beginnings of British sea power under Henry VIII, created as a defence after the break from Catholic Europe, and which led, in Elizabethan times, to exploration, an increase in trade and the emergence of a new class of merchants and 'gentry'. Rivalry with Spain in the 'New World' over trade resulted in the Armada of 1588, an event about which loyal British Roman Catholics felt ambivalent and which reflected conflicting loyalties and rivalries throughout Europe.

This unit allows children many opportunities to consider non-Eurocentric

L'ESCORIEL

2D

JULY 1588

HE MUCKED UP OUR -
INVASION PLAN

He Duke of Palma mucked up our invasion plan because he was not ready in Dunkruk to sail.

Philip II was very angry when he found out. On the other hand Philip was pleased with The Duke of Medina Sidonia because he had reached Calais not losing too many ships and not having a sea battle with Englande.

After this achievement, How did the Duke of Palma dare to say that his 17,000 men, 1000 cavalry, 170 ships would not be ready for 2 weeks.

Which side was God on?

I thought God was meant to be on our side

THE GOLDEN HIND

1gr

1st August 1588

ARMADA SIGHTED

It was two weeks ago at south of Eddy-stone Lighthouse that the Armada was spotted by the English Fleet. 1 week ago the English Fleet positioned themselves behind the Spainish Fleet and had the advantage of being windward. A couple of days ago the prize ship "San Salvardor" arrived at Weymouth badly damaged. We think that there was an explosion below decks. There were quite a few smoke blackened corpses on board.

Fight for Elizabeth.

—She is our Queen—

FIRE SHIPS

A plan to send out some fire ships to Calais harbour in France is still to be decided on for Queen Elizabeth is not sure whether it is a good idea.

and non-Anglocentric perspectives. Firstly, the competition between Britain and Spain to find new routes to India and the East Indies, and the ensuing conflict in Central America and the West Indies allows children to use sources which reflect both cross-cultural influences and cultural conflict. A Schools Council booklet 'Akbar and Elizabeth' (1983) shows teachers how they can help children to discover from Indian miniatures (in the Victoria and Albert Museum) the rich cultural influences of India on Elizabethan England by comparing clothes, buildings and garden design.

Often, sources which challenge Eurocentric perspectives can be selected from books for older children. In Roberts (1992, pp. 22–25) there are excellent Mughal pictures of the rejoicing at the birth of Jahangir, son of Akbar the Great in 1569. The relief at the birth of an heir and also the idealistic representation of

Mathematics

I learned Making
Tudor House Models.

length estimate measure	metres centimetre	I estimated the height of my house as 4m.
Scale	1:100	The lenght of my house in real life would be 12m and on my model it is 12cm
Convert from one unit to another.	metres to cm, cm to mm (to nearest mm)	The width of my house is 6m which on my model would be 6cm it could also be 6mm. 6m = 600cm = 6000mm
area rectangle triangle	cm² m²	the area of my first rectangle is 72cm². The area of my roof is 16cm²
Volume of cuboid	cm³ m³	The volume of my 2nd cuboid is 252cm³.
Properties of solid shapes Cuboid	faces edges angles	On a cuboid there is 6 faces 12 edges 24 angles
△ based prism	faces edges angles	5 faces 9 edges 12 angles
measuring angles right angle		the right angle on my roof is 90°. the right angle on the side of my roof is 90°
acute angle		there are 4 acute angle on my house. the acute angles are 45°
obtuse angle		there are 0 obtuse angles on my house.

this event suggests similarities both between portraits of Elizabeth and her succession problems. It is interesting too that when Sir James Ross arrived at the Court of Jahangir, the Emperor thought most of the gifts from Europe were poor but he did like an English miniature portrait of a Lady (a result of Indian influence on European art), and a map of India which he was given. However, Jahangir was not really interested in foreign rulers as he saw them as subordinates.

The Benin Empire was also at its peak at the same time as the Tudors were ruling England, which is when the British first arrived there. Sources about the Benin Kingdom can be found in the Museum of Mankind and the British Museum and through the Benin Society. They invite comparisons and contrasts with Tudor England; the mother of an Oba, or ruler, was of great importance, for example, and had her own palace and political power. Benin contained craft guilds of leather workers, weavers and blacksmiths. Written sources record its richly decorated palaces and houses. Extensive trade with Europe from the end of the fifteenth century included slaves. Smith (1992, p. 9) shows the crest of Sir John Hawkins, a successful English slave-trader of the sixteenth century, which he designed for himself and which depicts a defiant, captured African.

Similarly Green (1992) offers a picture of what life was like for the native peoples of the Americas, when Europeans first arrived and of how they perceived each other. For example, George Best who sailed with Martin Frobisher to North America wrote a detailed diary which is quoted, and there is also a contemporary painting of Frobisher's fight with an Inuit in 1577. From knowledge of such sources, children can develop a less Eurocentric and a more questioning attitude to life in Tudor times and view it from a range of perspectives.

As part of the focus on ships, both Year 5 and Year 6 spent two weeks finding out about the Armada. The competition between Britain and Spain to find new routes to India and the East Indies, and the ensuing conflict in central America and the West Indies, underlined by religious differences, was explained in class lessons. The viewpoints of different groups were discussed. How would the English Protestants feel, the English Catholics, the French, the Dutch, the Spanish? Why might the Scots be ambivalent? Children then worked in groups or individually to find out all they could about the daily progress of the Armada, making charts, maps and diaries. They made a display of daily rations for a Spanish and an English sailor, pie charts of the estimated food needed on a ship, and graphs showing ships of different kinds. Finally, each class worked in six groups together with the advisory teachers for Information Technology; by the end of a day, each group succeeded in producing a 'broadsheet' giving news of the Armada from the standpoint of a particular group. The French produced 'La Grenouille', the Spanish 'L'Escorial', the English Protestants 'The Golden Hind', the English Catholics 'the Priesthole' and the Scots 'the Record'.

Later, they evaluated the extent to which they had reflected different attitudes. These examples show that children are considering the reasons for behaviour and events.

The extracts from broadsheets representing different points of view were written on 'Armada Day'. They are based on 'press releases' and information in simulated teletext using 'Simtex', prepared by the Croydon Humanities adviser, Don Garman.

Models of Tudor timber-frame houses, based on particular examples, involved a range of mathematical concepts: measure, scale, properties of solid shapes. P.87 shows part of a child's self-evaluation sheet, made when he had finished his model, to explain the mathematics he thought he had learned in making it.

CHAPTER 5

Collaboration in Professional Development

In this chapter, three case studies describe how tutors, students, teachers and children worked together to explore new approaches to primary history. The first case study replaces the description of a residential weekend in the first edition of this book, which was based on the seventeenth century and is an optional but no longer a compulsory period of study at key stage 2. The new case study shows in detail how history students worked with teachers over half a term to organise and evaluate a 'Victorian Day' in a local house for key stage 1 children. The second case study describes a half-day workshop in which students experienced the processes of historical enquiry at their own level, then translated them into experiences suitable for children of different ages. The third describes a one-day workshop to introduce non-specialist primary school teachers to the kinds of historical thinking which underpin history in the National Curriculum. Since it seems unlikely that there will be a great deal of money available for in-service courses on primary history in the near future, these examples are given as ideas, based on experience, for workshops which groups of teachers could undertake for themselves.

THE MIREHOUSE PROJECT

There has been an increased emphasis in recent years on finding out about the past through reconstructions. These can involve all the key elements of historical thinking; finding out how the past was different by making inferences from a variety of sources and organising them to create an interpretation of what it might have been like. However, it is important to be aware that such reconstructions involve complex questions about the nature of historical imagination and historical empathy which are discussed in Chapter 6.

The Mirehouse Project can be seen in the context both of Living History Reconstructions organised by, for example, the Young National Trust Theatre and by English Heritage, and of projects organised by teachers. Examples of school-based history reconstruction projects can be found in Teaching History (e.g. Fleming, 1992, pp. 14–16; Tonge, 1993, pp. 25–29), in Primary History (e.g. Martin and Cobb, 1992, pp. 17–18), and in Young Historian Scheme Projects (e.g. Ferguson and Montgomerie, 1995). However, unlike the case study described, these all involve children at key stage 2.

Mirehouse is a yeoman's house on the shore of Lake Bassenthwaite in Cumbria. It dates from the seventeenth century, but was extended during the last century and most of the furnishings date from this time. It is well known for its connections with Alfred Lord Tennyson who was a friend of the owner James Spedding and stayed there twice in 1835 and 1850. The Spedding family still owns the house, which is open to the public, and were extremely generous in allowing a group of students to plan work with key stage 1 children based on the house in Victorian times.

The students involved had completed a one-year course in academic history, but had not previously worked with children on a history project.

I Planning for the Mirehouse Day: the organisational framework

Timetable

Week 1	Preparation for school-based work
Week 2	Work in school on Victorian topics in preparation for Mirehouse Day (Y1 and Y2)
Week 3	Students visit Mirehouse, to modify and develop plans for Mirehouse Day
Week 4	Tutorials to agree final plans for Mirehouse Day
Week 5	MIREHOUSE DAY
Week 6	Presentation and evaluation of work at Mirehouse

Aims of the project for students

a) To explore ways of teaching 5–7 year olds about the past through activities which develop genuine historical enquiry by:
   - using a variety of sources to make deductions and inferences about how things were made and used in the past, and their effects on the lives of people who used them;
   - understanding the ways in which the past was different, and also that some things do not change;
   - trying to reconstruct the past through role-play and so beginning to understand why there are different interpretations of the past.

b) To consider the preparation, organisation and follow-up of a visit to a historical site.

c) To evaluate teaching and children's learning.

Participating schools

A cluster group of five isolated and very small rural primary schools, which therefore particularly welcomed the opportunity to work with a larger group.

Context for role play

The family are returning to Mirehouse after their long summer holiday in 1894. (A precise date was important in order to establish which events and inventions had already occurred during the long Victorian period, and so to create roles and background for characters.) Children from the nearby village are helping to get the house ready for their return. At some points, the children are invited to join the family, in the nursery, the music room and the library, for lessons, stories and singing. It was seen as important that the children should be in role as both servants and friends of the family. This involved switching perspective in different activities. Although, as explained in Chapter 6, the development of historical imagination and empathy is a complex process, the children appeared able to understand that children in different situations had different experiences.

Role play activities devised for:

Q1   the nursery
A1   the verandah (washing, polishing, carpet beating)
Q2   the library
A2   the lawn/barn
A3   the music room
(Q = quiet; A = active)

Plan for groups: the Mirehouse Day

9.30   Students arrive.
        Prepare their role-play activities (3–4 students per activity).
10.00   Children arrive in barn; pattern for day outlined to them.
        Organised in groups of about 15, each with a teacher, also in role as a
        guest, to meet Mrs S. in role as the housekeeper.
10.15   Begin rotation of activities (each lasted 35 minutes).

During lunch time, a 'Victorian' photographer with a camera on a stand, concealed under a black cloth, takes individual photographs of the children. These are developed in sepia and used in school to compile marbled 'Victorian' albums, or display in shell-encrusted frames, as a basis for creative writing.

Diagram 5.1: *Programme for Mirehouse Day*

School	10.15–10.50	10.50–11.25	11.25–12.00	12.00–12.35	12.35–1.10	1.10–2.00
Ireby	Q1 Nursery	A1 Verandah	Q2 Library	LUNCH AND PHOTOS	A2 Lawn/Barn	A3 Music Room
Borrowdale	A1 Verandah	Q2 Library	A2 Lawn/Barn	LUNCH AND PHOTOS	A3 Music Room	Q1 Nursery
Bassenthwaite	Q2 Library	A2 Lawn/Barn	A3 Music Room	LUNCH AND PHOTOS	Q1 Nursery	A1 Verandah
Braithwaite	A2 Lawn/Barn	A3 Music Room	Q1 Nursery	LUNCH AND PHOTOS	A1 Verandah	Q2 Library
Bolton	A3 Music Room	Q1 Nursery	A1 Verandah	LUNCH AND PHOTOS	Q2 Library	A2 Lawn/Barn

II Preparing for a role; analysis of the process

1. Research key events in the life of the character, and in the lives of the people they live with and near.

2. Research what is known from sources about their personality, attitude, feelings.

3. Research background formation about the period relevant to the character, daily life, travel, clothes.

4. Build what is known into the planned reconstruction; what events can be referred to in conversation? What personal viewpoints, character can be expressed?

5. How can the skeleton knowledge of what is known from sources be developed and extended, based on what is likely? The interpretation is valid if it is compatible with what is known, and if there is no evidence to the contrary.

Example: preparation for the role of Audrey Boyle, wife of Hallam Tennyson, Lord Alfred Tennyson's elder son Researching and creating this role, raised awareness of the sensitive issues involved in writing biographies, particularly of those whose relatives may still be alive, in spite of the fact that this is the process through which history is written. The references are from Martin (1980). The tutor decided to develop this role because there are detailed records of Alfred Tennyson's visits to Mirehouse, although it is unlikely that his daughter-in-law would have visited – another example of what Elton (1970) saw as 'historical imagination, a tool for filling in the gaps when facts are not available'.

94

1894 Perspectives	*Key Dates*	
11 years ago	1883	Met Hallam Tennyson, aged 29, while staying with relatives at Freshwater – a beautiful, penniless Irish girl.
10 years ago	1884	June – married Hallam in Henry VII chapel, Westminster Abbey; a grand wedding, guests included Browning and Arnold. Emily Tennyson, the mother-in-law, was losing her favourite son and was ill, but attended in a bath chair. Hallam and Audrey were responsible for his parents until their deaths, sleeping in the next bedroom, and rarely dining alone. Audrey looked after her mother-in-law when Hallam and Alfred were away.
5 years ago	1889-4	2 sons born, eldest Leonard (second son a baby)
2 years ago	1892	Alfred Tennyson died. Audrey's role during his last week was to record all symptoms and conversation for Hallam's biography.
Background information		
60 years ago (20 years before Audrey was born)	1835	April and end of May – Alfred Tennyson visited Mirehouse, Fitzgerald (Rubaiyat) also guest of James Spedding who was son of local landowner. No railway. Stagecoach to Kendal, left 8am next day by coach to Keswick. Alfred adored the Lakes County but 'could dispense with the constant deluges of sapping rains. I understand the demon vapour descends there in constant drizzle' (letter to sister Emily). While at Mirehouse, the friends rowed on the lake, read and recited poetry before the library fire, took dogs for rambles over fells, and James Spedding sketched Tennyson (who also played chess with Mrs Spedding).
About 45 years ago	1850	Alfred visited Mirehouse with his new wife Emily. (James brought all the old socks he had discarded in his bachelor days in London and laid them, holes uppermost, on their bed.)
14 years ago	1881	March, James Spedding died. Hallam visited him in St Georges Hospital, London, but Alfred did not.
7 years ago	1887	Alfred Tennyson chartered Sir Allan Young's yacht, Stella, for a cruise of Wales, the West Country and Channel Islands. Hallam and Audrey went with him. Alfred Tennyson snubbed Dean of St David's Cathedral who attempted to show them round and invited them to tea.

Character

Apparently felt left out and that the intellectual level of the Tennyson house was rather too high for her. Her role in the household was negligible. She was embarrassed by Alfred (e.g. his dislike of Americans conveyed to John Chapman, a guest for lunch in 1880s who was a Harvard Graduate – Audrey gave him a torn page of the daily newspaper as a memento, in her agitation as he left!).

Reconstruction

In 1894, Audrey, Lady Hallam Tennyson, is about 36. She has a son of five and a younger son. Her elderly, sick mother-in-law, Emily Tennyson, depends on her. Her father-in-law, the eminent poet, died two years ago, aged 83. Audrey Tennyson is making a brief visit to the Speddings at Mire House (her father-in-law's old friend James Spedding had lived here but died 14 years ago) after the birth of her second child. Hallam had visited James Spedding at St George's Hospital in London during his final illness in 1881. Audrey has traveled by steam train to Keswick, unlike her father-in-law, who, on his first visit in 1835, came by coach to Kendal, then on the following day to Keswick. She is interested to see whether the 'demon vapour' will descend in continuous drizzle as he described. She is interested to see the chair where Alfred read poetry beside the library fire wearing his great cloak against the cold. Audrey Tennyson has much to talk about. For example, the time when James put the old socks on the elder Tennyson's marital bed in 1850 and how Hallam had visited James Spedding 15 years ago, three years before Audrey and Hallam were married. Audrey Tennyson chats to other guests about her cruise to the Channel Islands two years ago before Leonard was born, and compares this with her impressions of rowing on Bassenthwaite Lake. She talks about Leonard's birth (the fear, the pain and her rejection of chloroform). She refers to the constraints of her domestic life and describes in detail the last week of Alfred Tennyson's life.

Intervention opportunities: Audrey, Lady Hallam Tennyson

Nursery

Baby clothes and bath similar to those of Audrey's baby; toys and rocking horse would be enjoyed by five-year-old son, Leonard.

Library

Chair where father-in-law, Alfred, sat 50 years ago with James Spedding and

'Fitz' reading poetry.

Music room

Was this room built when her father-in-law Alfred first came in 1835, or was it built on his second visit in 1850?

Verandah

Audrey doesn't have much of a role in the Tennyson household in London therefore is very interested in 'below stairs' tasks.

Lawn

Audrey can see the lake where Alfred and James Spedding rowed in 1835 and the Fells they walked. Will the weather still be wet?

III Planning the activities

First, in small groups, the students planned activities to last for an afternoon, in each of the participating schools. The purpose of this was for them to become aware of the kinds of thinking in history that key stage 1 children are capable of in order to plan appropriate activities for the Mirehouse Day. In the light of this experience, each group planned an activity for the Victorian Day. They refined and modifed this after their visit to the house when they saw the rooms in which they would be working and discussed with Mrs S. which artefacts and furniture may be touched, which could only be looked at and what should be moved to a place of safety! They checked too what artefacts they needed to bring with them, how they could exploit those that were in the house, and what Mrs S. could provide. (This generously included a collection of Afghan rugs for the children to beat clean after they had been strewn with ash by the students for maximum effect!) Finally, the students were given a check list for reviewing their preparation.

Lesson plan check

● Have you developed a role for yourself: social status, occupation, gender, age, daily life, where you live, family, position in family, personality, previous events in your life? What are you doing at Mirehouse? What will you convey of this information to the children? How? (Body language, dress, information.)

● Have you found out some background knowledge about the period which is relevant to your activity in Mirehouse? What? How will you use this?

- Does the activity you planned exploit the unique Mirehouse environment: the house, furniture, paintings, artefacts? How?

- How will you help children to change their perspectives from 1994 to that of 1894? (e.g. to ignore things which have happened since then; to see the ways in which life was different and why).

- Do you have evidence that the activity you plan is based on what is known about the past? (e.g. did children in 1894 play leap-frog? How do you know?

- Does the activity reflect historical enquiry? Is it based on sources; what sources? Does it allow children to make deduction and inferences? Does it help them to see differences and similarities between (Mirehouse) now and in 1894?

- Have you planned the activity in sufficient detail: who will lead and who will support? How will you involve the teacher in the role? Will the group be subdivided? What will each of you say, do, ask, tell? How might you intervene during the activity? What is the timetable for your session?

- Can you evaluate to what extent learning objectives are achieved? For individual children or for the group? Through your questions, children's responses? (verbal responses or actions or through observation)

- Have you collected your resources; arranged how to transport you and them?

- Do you need to extend or modify your activity plan in the light of the above? If so, do so! Then you can enjoy the day (and repeat it elsewhere in different contexts!). You will have explored the key issues and cracked all the major challenges of teaching real history at key stage 1.

IV Students' preparation in school and related activities at Mirehouse

Group A

Work in school

Three activities for rotating groups to help children investigate how household chores were done 100 years ago, how things have changed and why. Each group in turn discuss a flat iron, a carpet-beater and a posher (dolly stick). They discuss how each was made and used, what it felt like to use it, what is used today, why this is different and how people's lives have changed as a result. They draw each artefact and identify it in visual sources.

Mirehouse activities, the verandah (barn if wet)

Three rotating activities involving domestic chores:

- washing clothes: fetching water from the stream washing rags and clothes; putting washing through the mangle; hanging washing on line; 'ironing clothes' (cold iron).

- carpet beating

- cleaning brass

Resources: buckets; dolly tub; posser (x 3); soap; washboard; washing line; wooden pegs; clothes to wash; ironing table; cloth and irons; carpet beaters; rugs (x 2); brass; cleaner; rags; aprons.
Organisation: we will play a housekeeper and two housemaids – Mrs Bridges, Tilly and Meg.

When the children arrive, the housekeeper will be telling the housemaids to get the washing done while she gets on with the cleaning. Tilly and Meg will ask the children if they could help them to do the washing, and the housekeeper would like a few children to help her with the cleaning. As the bigger group of children will be helping with the washing, we shall ask if the class teacher could help here also. When fetching water from the stream we would like the children to do it one at a time as the stream is quite low down and they may struggle when crouching to get the water in their buckets. We will also add warm water so that the washing water is not too cold. After a brief demonstration, we will get the children to help with the various processes of washing the clothes.We will try to ensure that there are always dry pieces of cloth for the children to iron and that there are enough things for each group to wash. The children who will be cleaning with 'Mrs Bridges' will be given aprons or shirts to keep them clean, and rags to clean the brass with. These children will be split so that they each have a turn at carpet beating and cleaning brass. If it is a rainy day and it is not really practical to do the cleaning on the verandah, we will set everything up in the barn and try to do all the activities in there. In conclusion, when it is time for each group to move on, we will thank them for their help and mention that the Spedding family will no doubt appreciate that all their washing and cleaning has been done.

Lady Tennyson's observations

Children who had clearly talked about their role at home were noticeably in role all day. One child whose face was soot-stained (and who brought home-made lemonade in a jam jar tied with string for his lunch), told me that before helping with the washing, which he enjoyed, he had been up a chimney. Meg, the maid, was heard to ask whether they liked using her nice new light iron which was much better than her other one and explaining that when she and Tilly had to do all the ironing on their own, they got it 'steaming hot' (it was a bit cooler today for the new helpers).

Group B

Work in school

Four activities for rotating groups to investigate and extend what children know about Victorian homes, books, behaviour at table and pastimes. In turn, each group will:

- compare a Victorian doll's house with a contemporary doll's house;
- compare examples of Victorian children's books with their own;
- compare rules for meal-time behaviour with their own experiences, using a nineteenth-century poem;
- colour characters for use in a Victorian toy theatre.

Mirehouse activities, the lawn (barn if wet)

Four rotating groups involving Victorian games (Opie and Opie, 1973):

- Blind Man's Buff with Beatrice a 'daughter of the house';
- skipping games and rhymes (taught by Rose, a lady's maid, on her day off);
- hop scotch (taught by the groom, on his day off, although he did check that the stable lad had fed and watered the horses at lunch time!);
- drilling and exercise under tuition of Albert, the gardener, who was 'let down by men who weren't fit', before he was invalided out of the Boer War of 1881. He doesn't intend Her Majesty, Queen Victoria, to be let down again by unfit young men.

Group C

Work in school

Rotating activities to find out and extend what children know about learning to read and count, sing and draw in Victorian times. In turn, each group will learn to recite the alphabet, to use an old abacus to do sums, to sing tonic sol-fa from a stave and to trace line-drawings of a pump, a spinning top and a cart horse taken from a nineteenth-century children's book.

Mirehouse activities, school room/nursery

- Drawing an object selected from an 'object box' (on slates);
- a hand-writing exercise using a sand box;
- reciting tables.

At the start of the session, the children will be asked to line up at the entrance to the school room. The governess and master will be very strict, liberal only with the cane and the dunce's hat. The lesson will end with the children's work being marked before they line up and file out.

Lady Tennyson's observations

Under the very austere direction of the tutor bearing his cane, and the governess, there was much emphasis on manners. 'Yes sir' and 'Please sir', and 'Speak when you're spoken to'. (When discipline was more rigorous than two little girls could bear, the tutor proved more upset than they were!) The date was copied from the blackboard, 7 November 1894, then an object lesson drawing half apples and labeling the parts was followed by alphabets and sums copied on to slates, or with letter formation practice in the sand tray, rewarded by rides on the rocking horse for the younger pupils. 'Did you wash behind your ears lad?' the teacher was heard to bark.

Group D

Work in school

Children will discuss a Victorian sampler; the text (a prayer), the date, the motifs; how it was made, by whom, and why. They will copy a motif and write their name in crosses on to squared paper, as a pattern for sewing a cross-stitch bookmark.

Mirehouse activities, library

Reading from a variety of Victorian children's books beside the fire in the library. This will be very discreetly video-recorded for assessment purposes, by a video camera placed under a silk shawl. (It was, in the event, so well concealed that during one session the scene was obscured by a teacher's large hat.)

Lady Tennyson's observations

The sisters wondered what colour their cousin's dress might be on a photograph she had sent them, and laughed about Uncle Rupert's top hat, which he had had for years. They found a coloured picture glued into the new book she had sent them, by post, but found, to their disappointment, that all the other pictures were black and white. The sisters taught the children a 'recently published rhyme' which they were amazed to find the children already knew. There was an interesting discussion in which the children told the sisters that they had come in a car. 'Is it like a horse?' the sisters asked. 'Does the coachman sit outside with a whip to make it go?' 'I've never seen one in Borrowdale', said Rose. 'What strange ideas you have, children.' There were discussions about whether children had a tea bell at home; the children claimed to know it was tea-time from a clock with a battery worn on the wrist, and confused the sisters by saying that they cut their own grass. 'Albert would not like us to interfere in our garden', they replied.

Group E

Work in school

Children use Christmas card pictures of a 'Victorian Christmas' and compare it with their own; what is the same, what is different and why? Was it really like this? Compare with variety of pictures of poor Victorian homes, in reference books.

Mirehouse activities, Music room

We will be in role as members of a Victorian family. As the children enter the room they will view us reading, sewing or chatting. We will express surprise and pleasure at the children's arrival. The children will be invited to sit on the rug and we will sit facing them on the sofa. We will ask questions about where the children have travelled from and how they have travelled. We will build up our own roles, talking about a recent visit to London and express a lack of knowledge about their form of travel. We will ask the children if they will play one of our favourite games – I Spy. This will enable us to focus upon certain aspects of the room, make points about them and pick up on children's anachronistic comments. For example, we will look at the fire, paintings, books and piano. In role, we will then be able to respond to any questions the children might have and encourage them to think about Victorian pastimes. We will ask what Victorian songs they know (i.e. do they know any songs that we know?). We will teach the children songs such as 'Pat-a-cake' from the *Oxford Nursery Rhyme Book*, and the *Oxford Dictionary of Nursery Rhymes*, (1951), both by Iona and Peter Opie. We will conclude with Victorian songs the children have already learned in school.

Lady Tennyson's observations

The three house guests explained that they had arrived by carriage. They chatted to the children about the coal fire, the coal bucket and bellows. Some children said they had such a fire at home but others confusingly claimed to have 'hot wires' that 'worked like a kettle'. After a game of 'I Spy', the children played other parlour games with great pleasure. Some of them claimed to have the songs 'on a tape' at home – very confusing to the grown ups.

IV Mirehouse evaluation

Some observations on the value of role-play and on the importance of an authentic environment for development of young children's historical understanding.

To what extent could the children change perspectives?

Some of the children in the school room were terrified by the severity of the master (who was more upset by this than they were), whereas they relished being drilled by the Boer War veteran although he was equally fierce. They were familiar with school, reading and sums and did not know such a different experience of school was possible. Because the role-play situation was parallel to their own experience they could not all transfer perspectives and respond in role; the role-play did not alter their expectations and responses. By contrast, they enjoyed the military drilling because they knew that soldiers are treated in this way and so could respond in role. In free play, children often play soldiers. It reflects their need to explore adult situations and gender roles, power and control in a safe environment. Because there is a clear change of perspectives, and move from reality to fantasy, they are also free to move in and out of role as they need·to and to reject experiences they cannot handle. Sometimes the marching became a little levitous, other commands were received with a frisson of fear! Therefore, should role-play situations for young children be in a situation markedly different from their own, or is it only necessary to give children more knowledge about how the past was different before they go into role?

How important is an authentic environment for role-play in historical contexts?

The photographs showed in a very revealing way the impact of the gracious and spacious Victorian environment on everyone who participated. Speech and body language for adults and children were influenced by sitting in a large chair, before a roaring fire and holding a precious book or an embroidery frame. Oranges and Lemons is rarely so decorously played. Scrubbing linen with water collected from a real stream and pegging it out on a cold windy day produced quite different gestures and reflected genuinely different feelings. This confirmed the view of Garvey (1977) that through dressing up (and, by extension, being in a related environment), children do not merely illustrate what they have known, observed and experienced, but try on different hats, look at themselves in the mirror and interpret the feelings and behaviour of the image they see which is remote from their direct experience.

Some further questions

- Did the role-play continue in school?

- Did it develop a narrative element? What was the stimulus for this? Were there links between the children's own lives and concerns, and the historical context for exploring them?

- How did the children integrate into the play the knowledge they had acquired at Mirehouse? Did they use the new vocabulary they had learned? Did the role-play lead to further investigations?

- Could more poems have been found which would help children understand the ways in which the past was different, and which could be linked with the role-play? For example, Little Orphan Annie, by James Whitcomb Riley, published in the Indianapolis Journal, 1885, describes the life of a child servant who is given 'board and keep' to 'shoo the chickens off the porch', 'dust the hearth and sweep'. It refers to the 'lampwick splutters' and the 'chimbley flue', making the fire and baking the bread.

'The Dolls Wash', by Julian Horatia Ewing, first published in *Aunty Judy's Magazine*, September 1874, describes in detail a Victorian washday which the children replicate in washing their dolls' clothes. Sally has tubs and a copper in the wash house, and a great big fire and plenty of soap, and outside is the drying ground with tall posts and pegs bought from the gypsies and long lines of rope.

Robert Louis Stevenson's poems describe lamp-lighters, candles, firesides, and the excitement of the new steam train. All of these poems were found in the *Oxford Book of Children's Verse* (Opie and Opie, 1973).

V Transfer to another site

Although the experience had shown what benefits role-play can have for key stage 1 history, it would be difficult to replicate a similar day as a teacher. The organisation was considerable. Students might therefore:

i)   use a similar 'ready-made' living history experience at a site;

ii)   use the experience to initiate and support play, in a historical context, in the classroom;

iii) if in a large school, work with other classes in the school on a Victorian Day, a Tudor Day or a Medieval Day;

iv) if the school were part of a consortium with a strong history coordinator, such a project, involving schools in the consortium would be possible.

Suggestions for future projects: links between work in school and at Mirehouse

i) Schools could give parents more information about the purpose of the project and how to support their children 'in role'. It was noted that children who were most 'in role' were those whose parents had encouraged this at home.

ii) If the schools were clearer what preparation was helpful before the day, they would be more confident in providing this; e.g. some information about Victorian schools so that children would not be upset by their severity.

iii) One school had sent parents a follow-up questionnaire to involve them in the project.

Organisation of the day

i) Students would like to know what other groups were doing. Could they demonstrate to each other beforehand? Could they have a video made to watch afterwards?

ii) Timing would be helped by a bell (servants bell?) built in to 'plot' as a signal to move on. The 'plot' could have been developed to create a coherent rationale for changes. Or teachers could have been used to make the links and act as prompts.

iii) Some students would have liked longer on each activity so that they could build more of their researched role in to the talk with children.

A HALF DAY WORKSHOP

The aim of this workshop was to introduce the group (of PGCE students) to the various strands of historical thinking, the key elements of the National Curriculum, through interpreting a range of sources at their own level of enquiry, then considering how to plan similar activities suitable for children at key stage 1 or 2. In order to focus students' thinking on the past before the workshop, to involve them in problem-solving which was rooted in their own experiences and interests but did not involve too much preparation, and also to encourage them to get to know something of each other, they had been asked to 'bring in something as old as you, or older'. Before they arrived, a table was covered with attractive drapes and a small but visibly stimulating collection of the tutor's personal artefacts was set out, to which people responded and added their own contributions as they arrived. This was a marvellous ice-breaker, as family photos and heirlooms, things dug up in gardens, or found in junk shops were explained, demonstrated and speculated upon. This led on to a discussion of the wide-ranging nature of historical sources and the questions which can be asked about them. The discussion involved ideas of certainty, probability and accepting that some things may never be known; key questions such as how it was made, when and where and why; supporting and contradictory evidence, the status of evidence, and range of interpretations possible at different levels of likelihood, about causes and effects, and the relationship between evidence and the thoughts, feelings and behaviour of people. Then ways of introducing the concept of historical evidence to children were considered, such as 'dustbin clues' (what can we deduce from its contents. . .?), burying a box (what shall we put in it?), or finding a suitcase in an attic (what does it tell us about the owner?).

Some students later introduced work in history with children by an evidence exercise. John Fusco, introducing work on transport, asked Year 5 children to put things into an imaginary box which could tell a museum owner in a hundred year's time about how we travel in 1991. He found that at first they chose only visual evidence related to their own experience, (a seat belt 'to show we cared about safety', roller skates, model cars and magazine advertisements). When he asked them what sort of a picture this would give, they found it difficult to realise that the museum owner would not have the same knowledge as we have today, but gradually came to see that their collection was selective. They then added photographs of a Rolls Royce and of Concorde, explaining that 'this is how rich people travel', and a lifejacket and an anchor to reflect travel by sea, although they had no experience of this. They also began to propose some written records – a Highway Code and a road map, newspaper articles on a new model of car, and an account of a family cycling around the world. At first the children thought that the deductions which could be drawn in a hundred year's time were factual and descriptive, the colour and shape of cars, or how many people can get on a train, but with prompting they began to consider the attitudes and values, thoughts and feelings which might lie behind the artefacts; would people understand that Reebok trainers are very expensive, and a status symbol amongst children?

Key stage 1, group 1, oral history

This group was given a tape-recording of an elderly lady's memories, supported by an album of photographs of her throughout her life. Students chose to listen to one of three sections: either 'childhood', or 'high school, university and early teaching career in the 1920s', or 'the evacuation of children during World War II'. They were told to listen to the tape either from the point of view of children (what questions might they ask, and how might they follow up such a session?), or at their own level. It was interesting that different groups, responding at their own level, focused on different aspects but all were incredulous that married women were not allowed to continue to teach (they found it hard to suggest any possible reason), that college students had to wear berets and be indoors at nine o'clock, and that when a young teacher from a poor family, struggling with a reception class of 50 in her first term, caught pneumonia and died in her lodgings, her headmistress's response was, 'The girl deserved it. She didn't wear woollen combinations.' They were also amazed that this lady had met her former pupils, now all old-age pensioners, at a reunion, the first for over fifty years. One of them had apologised, in tears, for her bad behaviour in class, but explained that she had been abused by her father – an insight her young teacher certainly didn't have in 1932.

Anne-Marie Devereux-Cooke, a KS 1 student, decided later to use an oral history approach with Year 1 children. They listened to two accounts of life during the Second World War. The first was a taperecording of life in a small town in Scotland, and the second was a talk given by a lady who had been a nurse during the London Blitz. The student was particularly interested in some small children's anxiety at being questioned about the accounts individually afterwards, whereas in a group they were able to share their ideas and develop them more confidently. She discussed with the children words particular to the period which had been used (roof-watchers, siren, netting, cables, search lights, home guard), and was surprised by the ability of some children, when the words were focused on, both to work out and explain their meaning, and also to correct misunderstandings revealed by other children.

Cables

Joanne	'They were for when the balloons blew up into the sky. . .and the cables hung down from the balloon, like that.'
Teacher	'And what were they for?'
Amiar	'To kill them.'
Danielle	'No, to make sure the aeroplanes don't come too close. . .'
Joanne	'The home guard was for watching the. . .'
James	'The aeroplanes.'
	'To protect you... to protect houses. . .'

In responding to the photographs which one of the ladies, Mrs Isaacs, brought to support her talk (pictures of her wedding, and of her son, born at the end of the war), these five-year-olds spontaneously used time vocabulary.

Joanne	'That was when you were young.'
James	'Not old like you are now.'
Amiar	'Is he a man now?'
Danielle	'Yes, it was a long time ago.'

The children frequently interjected with questions, to gain more information, to clarify and to determine validity. When Mrs Isaacs told them about an incident when her husband had been driving an ambulance in France which went over a landmine and was tossed in the air, James asked:

	'Did the other people in the van were they killed?'
Mrs Isaacs	'Quite a number. I don't know exactly how many. I wasn't there.'
James	'But how do you know if you weren't there? Did he tell you?'
Mrs Isaacs	'I didn't know until I received a letter from him.'
James	'He wrote a letter back, telling you he weren't dead?'
Mrs Isaacs	'That's right.'

Later, the children compiled a questionnaire for Mrs Isaacs of questions which were prompted by her talk. They responded much more actively to this talk than they did to the tape-recording because they were able to interact. However, the children did wonder why the two accounts were so different.

Joanne	'They both lived in World War 11. Why didn't she (Mrs Wilcockson) say all about the war like Mrs Isaacs did?'
James	'Because they both lived in different countries.'

They concluded that 'we don't have ration books now', or 'tin hats to protect ourselves, or wear gas masks'.

Key stage 1, group 2, artefacts

This group was asked to make an attractive 'museum display' of the artefacts and photographs contributed, then to list questions they would like to know about them (e.g. what they were, how they worked, who used them, why), and to try to answer them by asking their owners, or by using secondary sources in the library. They could then write a quiz about the exhibits for other students, write explanatory labels or a brochure to accompany the exhibition, or prepare an oral presentation for the end of the session. They were also asked to attempt to sequence the artefacts. Several students subsequently investigated children's ability to make deductions about artefacts, and to sequence artefacts and photographs. Susan Mead investigated the ability of four-year-olds to differentiate between an old and a new doll, and an old and a new teddy, after listening to a story about an old teddy. They concluded that one doll was new because 'she is hard plastic', while the old doll had a china head and a soft body 'full of fluff'. The teddy in the story says that 'you have to come from somewhere to have relatives' and Adam said, 'Everyone has a life-story. It means when you're a baby it starts.'

The teacher then went on to see if they could make 'family snakes' by writing the name of each family member on a flag, and sticking the flags into plasticine snakes, in sequence from the oldest to the youngest. Although the sequences had no clear order, Adam, for instance, grouped the 'nanny' flags together and insisted on one for the unborn baby at the other end of his snake.

Another student, Catherine Rigby, encouraged Year 5 children to make inferences about sources related to a Victorian topic. She gave them Victorian steel pens, a Victorian inkwell and a page from a copperplate copy book and asked them to practice writing the letters. They were enthusiastic. 'You're not like other teachers, you let us touch things without shouting at us.' Using the pens raised questions and led to discussion. One child spontaneously enacted how the monitors would have distributed the ink; this was information learned in a previous session. The children were voluntarily silent for a while, listening to the amazing noise of the nibs on the paper. They worked out how the ink was regulated by different nibs and wrote with uncharacteristic concentration. In another session, they were shown my grandmother's Victorian school time-table, with many hours allocated to needlework ('daylight permitting'), and to religious education, and they were shown a sampler. This led to a diverting discussion of religious beliefs, the amazing discovery that people could make their own clothes, and the observation that today some posters and stickers fulfil a similar purpose to that of sampler messages such as 'Charity begins at home'. They then went on to design and make their own samplers. This was a most surprising level of commitment from an extremely 'difficult' group of children.

Key stage 2, group 3, information technology data bases

The nature of a simple data-base programme was explained. It involves collecting information (records), with shared characteristics (fields), in order to look for patterns and trends. These can be recorded graphically as pie or bar charts, graphs or venn diagrams. We then considered the role of data bases in historical problem-solving. Firstly we listed the kinds of historical sources which could best be organised in this way:

(1) street directories, census and parish records of births, deaths, age, sex, occupation, address;

(2) other statistics relating to population (illness, height, diet);

(3) trade figures (cattle sold at Smithfield, price, weight, numbers);

(4) information about buildings or archaeological sites with some shared characteristics (e.g. plans of Roman villas, recording shape, size, hypercausts, mosaic pavements);

(5) place-name endings in an area indicating time and date of settlement (Roman, Viking, Saxon).

Secondly, we discussed how such information could be investigated through asking questions about change and about the causes and effects of change and interpreting the findings in the light of incomplete evidence, uncertainty, probability and what is known of the period. Thirdly, strategies were considered for involving a whole class of children in constructing and interrogating a data base. Each child can collect information for at least one record, complete a 'record sheet' on paper, categorising the information in fields to ensure that s/he can structure the information in this way, then type the record onto the data base. Next, when all the information has been collected, each child can fill in a second sheet setting out a question and the correct format for asking this question of the data base. When children have the responses to their questions they can fill in the last part of the sheet, saying what inferences they can make from them. This tried and tested method ensures that everyone understands how to use the data base, and has equal access to creating and interrogating it in a short time, although the complexity of the questions and sophistication of the deductions can vary considerably.

After this introduction, the group divided to return with their findings at the end of the session. One group spent the morning in a nearby churchyard collecting information from gravestones to put into an 'Our Facts' program (Anita Straker. MEP/MESU Primary Project). The other interrogated a ready-made data base on the Croydon and Stockport work houses (Community Information Resource Project. Croydon Advisory Service), compiled by a group of teachers for use at a range of levels, and supported by accompanying documentary evidence. This could fit in well with a Victorian project. One interesting finding was that most of the inmates were described as paupers; one of the few other groups was 'female school teachers'. Deductions? Another finding was that there were few girls in the work house but a lot of young boys. Reasons?

Key stage 2, group 4, portraits and written sources

Students were given portraits of Elizabeth I and of Horatio Nelson, and conflicting written sources related to each portrait. They were asked how valid the portraits are, as historical evidence. The sources were:

(a) (i) The 'Ditchley' portrait of Elizabeth I *c.* 1592 painted by Marcus Gheeraerts.
  (ii) Secondary sources explaining the circumstances in which it was painted and explaining the symbolism and imagery in the portrait: the purity of the eternally youthful virgin queen, the faery queen of pageantry, dominating a map of England and synonymous with it, banishing clouds and ushering in sunshine, her earring an armillary sphere symbolising the elements of God's created universe, and carrying a Protestant bible (Strong, 1987; Gittings, 1991).
  (iii) Contemporary descriptions of Elizabeth at about this time: Francesco Gradenigo 1596
  'Short and ruddy in complexion, very strongly built'
  M. de Maisse 1597
  'old, her face being long and thin, her teeth yellow and decayed but her figure is fair and tall and graceful in whatever she does. '
  Paul Hentzner 1598
  'fair but wrinkled, her eyes small yet black and pleasant, her nose a little hooked...her hair an auburn colour but false... '
(b) (i) Portrait of Horatio Nelson painted after the Battle of the Nile.
  (ii) Letter from Lord Nelson explaining how it had been commissioned, as a commemorative painting (Nelson Letters, 1971, Everyman, pp.195-7).
  (iii) Secondary source describing the ferocity and bloodiness of the battle (Pocock, 1974, 1987).

It was interesting that history graduates in the group found this exercise difficult. Unlike children, they felt that they should have a vast body of knowledge to bring to bear on the problem, and several of them also said that as undergraduates they had never worked with sources; they had only compared accounts of professional historians. Some of them, for the first time, raised questions about the nature of history.

The students became very keen to try using written and pictorial sources with children. John Fusco gave Year 5 children working on land transport an 1845 poster advertising an omnibus service from Colne and Burnley to Blackpool. He observed the inferences they made, the strategies they used, how they developed their ideas through discussion, and the kind of questions which helped them to do this. Daniel recognised the selectivity of the evidence, 'It's called The Safety... They're trying to make people think it's safe to travel like that, but it might be dangerous... ', Susan could make a valid inference about attitudes in society at the time. She didn't like seeing the horses whipped, but since 'they're showing them whipping them, nobody else must have minded'. The children were also very interested to argue about the meaning of the text. What was meant by 'obedient servants', by 'viz.', by 'Sea Bathing'? In another session, they were given an engraving by Dore of Ludgate Circus in 1872. Here, the children discussed the noise and crowds, and the speed of the traffic. They noticed that it was all either steam or horse-powered, and wondered how the street lamps worked. They noticed differences in the clothes of people in buses and carriages and the clothes of people on foot. They developed and contested each other's statements and recognised the incompleteness of the evidence: 'You can't tell what he's saying so you don't know if you're right.' They also noticed similarities with the present: 'I've seen a man in Tottenham Court Road with a placard like that.'

Key stage 2, group 5, the locality

Maps, directories, census records, engravings and photographs, newspaper accounts, buildings and street names
A range of records obtained from the local history library focused on three periods: the beginning, the middle and the end of the last century. They all referred to the immediate locality of the college. It was possible to trace changes. At the beginning of the century this was a rural environment with farms, streams and windmills. It was inhabited by whip makers, brewers and smiths and linked by the turnpike road to London and the coast. Then came the building of the railway at New Cross, with brick yards supporting the accompanying building development. This led to different social classes moving into the area by the end of the century ('independent gentlemen', chemists, grocers, engineers, surveyors, clerks, servants and labourers), whose places of origin were recorded in the census.

In giving such a range of documents to children, there would have to be clear groupings and precise questions. However, the adults selected their own enquiries. Some went off with cameras to take photographs from the same position today and compare similarities and differences. They found the site of the windmill at Thornville Street for example, and of the toll gate at the junction of Queens Road and New Cross Road. They stood where Lewisham High Road had once been photographed, splendid with carriages and gas lamps. Can we find the mews where the horses were kept? Is the gas fitting still on the wall?

Some went in search of 'older people' and asked them about the beginning of this century (they even returned with an elderly resident!). Some chose particular buildings and traced their occupants in a particular year last century, as a basis for supposing what life might have been like in the house then. Why did the 37-year-old wine merchant come from Spalding in Lincolnshire, offer lodgings to three scholars from Deptford, and to his 20-year-old wine merchant assistant, and employ a nursemaid of 17 from Market Rasen, at 44 Lewisham High Road in 1881? How did the 31-year-old chemist from Ireland come to live with his older French wife and his four infant children at number 56? What were their homes like, their clothes, their food, and what happened next? What did their road look like in the early photographs? Other students listed changes on three successive maps.

Linda Benton went on to do a similar exercise with Year 5 children, tracing changes in the locality of their school, through maps. She was amazed at how interested the children were and how well they were able to relate the observed environment to maps, to trace changes, and to relate maps to photographs, gravestone surveys, and written and oral accounts.

A ONE DAY WORKSHOP

The aim of this workshop was to introduce non-specialist primary school teachers to the thinking processes of historical problem-solving so that they could apply the National Curriculum attainment targets to KS 2 core study unit 1, Romans, Anglo-Saxons and Vikings in Britain, and so plan their own content and strategies for teaching this unit to children. A tall order in a short time!

To begin the day, three primary school history co-ordinators gave a brief overview of the Romans, Anglo-Saxons and Vikings, supported by maps, slides, and written primary and secondary sources. This gave the teachers basic information about where each of these groups came from, when and why, and told them something of their ways of life.

During the second part of the morning, teachers worked in groups to make time-lines for 100BC to 1000AD, to show different aspects of change. Two time-lines sequenced key events. (It was felt that this would give the opportunity to see that people have different reasons for what they select as 'key' events, that events cannot always be accurately dated, and that they represent different degrees of change.) The other time-lines showed clothes, buildings and domestic artefacts, agriculture and transport. Teachers were introduced to the idea of a time-line as a device for sequencing, for describing and explaining change, and the causes and effects of change, for observing and explaining similarities and differences and for cross-referencing change and different rates of change in different aspects of society. It was made clear that they can be made in different ways and interpreted at a range of levels. They may be made by individuals, or by a group; they may be small or span the length of a hall or corridor. They may be friezes on a wall, lines on a ceiling or 'linen lines' with pegs. They may be illustrated by writing, pictures or models, suspended from the ceiling, or displayed on bench tops. They may cover periods of different lengths. They may show sequence or precise dates; they may be to scale or not and are not necessarily linear.

Because time was short, teachers were asked to (photo)copy illustrations for their time-lines (whereas children would draw, or make models, or describe and explain in writing). A large variety of recently published materials was available: books, posters, postcards, slides, brochures about sites, museum publications. Teachers were introduced to this by using it for a particular purpose. They therefore became familiar with it, evaluated it, discussed it and cross-referenced it in double-quick time.

Everyone worked zealously! By the end of the morning, two large rooms were dripping with illustrations of changes in Britain from 100BC to 1000AD. As in any active learning situation, cueing from tutors was important, as the time-lines were being made; it was often important to explain that the problems arising were the essential nature of historical thinking. How far can you generalise from one example? What does one Viking longship in a museum represent? How far can you date change precisely? When did the Roman Empire end in Britain? Do all aspects of life change at the same rate? Did farming change under the Romans? What is development? Were the Romans more 'advanced' than the Saxons? Did these changes affect everybody? Did the Britons continue to live in Iron Age huts during the whole of the Roman period? Why did the Saxons become Christians? At first, people were confused and frustrated by such questions thrown up by the exercise.

Their presentation of the time-lines at the end of the session however, showed that they had begun to find the questions intriguing. The discussions they gave rise to were animated and teachers wanted to find out more. They had begun to understand what history is about.

The afternoon focused on the Roman period, since it was felt that people would be most confident about this. Teachers worked in groups to consider what different sources could tell us about the Romans: (secondary school classics courses provide useful documentation).

   (i) Written evidence: (a)   description of Caesar's landing in Britain, 26 August 55BC (De Bello Gallico IV.23)
                                       (b)   description of Boudicca from Tacitus' Annals XIV 29–34.
  (ii) Roman pottery found in the area, borrowed from a local museum. The curator explained where it was thought to have come from and its status. Rather coarse roof tiles, for example, represent a building of status in Roman Britain.
 (iii) Plan of the Roman Villa at Lullingstone.

(iv) Map of South East England in Roman times showing roads, towns and forts, tribes, tracks, iron workings, wooded areas and escarpments.

(v) Detail of frieze from the Great Dish, Mildenhall. British Museum slide PRB 47.

(vi) Shield boss found in the River Tyne (BM slide).

There was much discussion about what could be worked out, and also the limitations of each of the sources. People were surprised by the immediacy of the description of Boudicca:

> She was a huge woman, with a piercing gaze and strident voice. A mane of chestnut hair hung below her waist. Round her neck was a great golden torque. She wore a full, flowing tartan dress, and over it a thick cloak fastened by a brooch. She grasped a spear to terrify everyone.

How true is Tacitus' description? There were lively arguments about the veracity of Caesar's account of his landing

In the final session of the day, teachers considered the ways in which the key elements of the National Curriculum were reflected in the day's work. Then they were given a selection of formats for planning a study unit, relating resources to activities and key elements, which they filled in over the following weeks. The range of plans they submitted which were collated as a shared resource were encouraging in their variety. The best advice seems to be, do not try to do each study unit in equal depth. Within a study unit, get an overview of key events and changes by introducing time-lines and time vocabulary and asking questions about why things might have changed. Then select a few examples of key evidence, preferably related to a visit, which can be used as clues to find out more about the period. Finally, decide on how the findings might be organised, presented and explained to an audience, for example, through a museum exhibition, a slide show, a dramatic reconstruction or a tape-recorded 'radio programme'

CHAPTER 6

The National Curriculum and Action Research

As has been said earlier in this book, little is known about the levels of historical thinking which primary school children are capable of achieving. The National Curriculum is still no more than an initial attempt to provide a structure for promoting development in historical thinking. Research has suggested that monitoring children's development in history is particularly difficult because of interdependent influences: the nature of the evidence, the questions asked of it, and the teaching strategies used. This is now recognised in the key elements and level descriptions which are only broadly hierarchical and take into account children's thinking in a range of contexts. Any refinement in our understanding of children's historical thinking which will inform good practice will depend on building up banks of shared information about what children can do. Blyth, in *Making the Grade in Primary Humanities* (1990) emphasised the need for teachers to meet, both horizontally across their age range, and vertically in cross-phase groups to share ideas support each other, plan, discuss and evaluate. They may, for example, devise shared teaching plans for a unit of study across the same year group in a number of schools and compare children's responses, or combine to plan a local study across different year groups in order to plan for and monitor progression.

This Chapter will consider research done over two consecutive years as a class teacher of Year 3 children (Cooper, 1991), partly because it may offer some insights into teaching strategies and their effects, and also to encourage busy class teachers to consider action research as an inbuilt part of their approach to National Curriculum history. For already, the National Curriculum has been modified in the light of teachers' experience as the National Working Group Final Report (1990, pp. 175–6) and the then, Secretary of State intended (AMMA, 1990).

THE RESEARCH DESIGN

This investigates the hypothesis that young children can become involved in historical problem-solving, that there is a sequence in the early stages of their thinking which can be evaluated, that teaching strategies are significant in developing children's historical thinking, and that consistent teaching strategies can accelerate this development.

The research was undertaken in two primary schools in an outer suburb of south London. The following extracts of a discussion amongst eight-year-old children, about the Iron Age chalk horse at Uffington in Berkshire, give an introductory flavour of the study. It is interesting to compare them with the definition of a horse required by Mr Gradgrind, in the introduction to this book.

'It looks like a bird.'
'It's a horse.'
'They could draw horses.'
'So they had horses.'
'They were hard workers. . .skilful. . .artistic. . .'

'There must be a lot of chalk near the surface.'
'So there wouldn't be trees like oak trees here – not many trees.'
'They could live on the chalk – it's well-drained – the water would run away.'

'The soil would be thin – easy to plough.'
'Whatever tools they used, they must have been able to dig down into the ground to get to the chalk.'
'It must have taken a long time to make – maybe centuries.' 'They were hard workers. . .skilful. . .artistic. . .'
'They co-operated.'
'They lived in a community.'
'It's not an ordinary horse. It's much different from the ones we see.' 'It must be a special one or they wouldn't go to all that trouble.'
'It's probably a symbol for something – a clue.'
'To bring a good harvest?'
'A symbol of strength?'
'To an enemy? Perhaps the horse brought bad luck so they stayed away.'
'Perhaps if someone was ill they prayed to it. It gave them power when they were ill.'
'Or perhaps they just did it for fun.'
'Maybe they danced around it - or put fires on it and burnt something maybe for the chief's birthday.'
'I don't think they had birthdays.'
'But they had beliefs and ceremonies.'
'Customs.'

These children discuss the geology and the social organisation needed to make the horse, its practical and symbolic significance. They follow through and weigh each other's points. They synthesise them using abstract concepts: co-operate, community, ceremonies, beliefs, customs. They make a distinction between what they know and what they can only speculate about.

Two 'experimental' classes of Year 4 children were taught during consecutive years using carefully defined and documented teaching strategies and compared with a control group in another school taught by an experienced teacher using his own methods. The three groups were initially compared for ability by analyses of variance and covariance using NFER Non-Verbal Reasoning Test BD as covariate. All three groups were taught the same 4 units of history: the Stone Age, the Iron Age, the Romans and the Saxons, each unit lasting half a term. Each unit was taught within an integrated curriculum with a historical focus. About two hours each week were spent specifically on history.

The teaching strategies for the experimental groups involved discussion of key evidence, differentiating between what you could know 'for certain', what reasonable 'guesses' you could make, and what you 'would like to know' about the evidence. The discussion involved selected key concepts of different levels of abstraction (e.g. arrow, weapon, defence). Each unit of study involved one visit to a local area where there was evidence of settlement at each period and one 'further afield' visit to extend beyond the locality. For example, the Stone Age 'further afield' visit was to Grimes Graves, and the Roman one was to Lullingstone Roman Villa.

At the end of each unit, all three groups took five written 'evidence tests' which each lasted about half-an-hour on consecutive days. In each unit these consisted of five different types of evidence about which children had to make inferences: an artefact (or slide of one), a picture, a diagram, a map and written evidence. The aim was to investigate whether they found 'concrete' evidence more difficult to interpret than more abstract maps and written evidence. A list of evidence used is given in Table 6.1.

The experimental groups were also given an oral 'evidence test'. The children made a tape-recording of a discussion of each piece of evidence in small groups. During the first year the discussions were led by the teacher, and during the following year, no adult was present.

In addition, the second experimental group was given a storywriting test. They were given a piece of evidence related to the topic which was concerned with religion, beliefs, myth and ritual, so that it invited the children to piece together their knowledge into a coherent picture of the past and to attempt to consider and explain the beliefs and ideas of the period.

An assessment scheme on a ten-point scale was devised for the evidence tests. This was constructed from patterns in the development of deductive reasoning defined in cognitive psychology and in previous research relating this to history. It is not possible to quote it in detail, but it ranges from:

Table 6.1: *Evidence used in written and oral evidence tests*

Unit	Test 1 Artefact	Test 2 Picture	Test 3 Diagram	Test 4 Map	Test 5 Writing
1	Slide. Palaeolithic flint hard axes c. 200,000BC Museum of London. Slide OL91	Slide. Font de Gaume Lascaux. Ray Delvert S. Lot.	Stone circle. The Druids Circle. Caernarvon. Stone circles of the British Isles. A. Burle	Map showing site of neolithic artefacts on North Downs	Petroglyphics from 'How Writing Began' Macdonald
2	Bronze helmet (1BC) Slide BM	Uffington Horse photos	Little Woodbury, Iron Age house plan Wilts. In Cunliffe, R.K. 1974	Lynchets of Iron Age Fields Butser Hill, Hants.	Strabo 1.4.2. Description of British exports
3	Shield boss found in River Tyne. Slide BM.	Detail from frieze of great dish, Mildenhall Slide BM PRB 47	Villa plan Chedworth, Gloucs.	Roman roads across South Downs	Tacitus Annales XII 31–40 Boudicca Revolt
4	Replica of Sceptre. Sutton Hoo ship burial. BM Slide MZ 18	Illuminated manuscript of Harvest made by BM F21985	Plan Saxon church Cirencester	Saxon settlements in Surrey	Beowulf slays Grendel Penguin 1973 trans 824-838

level 1 – illogical;

level 2 – incipient logic not clearly expressed;

level 3 – restatement of information given;

levels 4 and 5 – one or two statements going beyond the information given;

level 6 – an attempted sequential statement inadequately expressed; *levels 7 and 8* – one or two logical sequential statements, where the second statement is based on the first, connected by 'therefore' or 'because';

levels 9 and 10 – a synopsis of previous points, using an abstract concept.

For example, given a map of an area of the North Downs where Stone Age implements have been found, a typical level 3 answer is 'There are clay areas, and chalk areas and steep slopes,' (which are given on the map). A level 4 statement is 'They had rivers to get water from.' An example of a level 8 statement is 'Chalky ground is not wet, therefore the tools are found there because Stone Age people could live there. And they were near a river, so they could get water to drink.' An example of a level 10 statement refers to a diagram of an Iron Age hut: 'They had huts. Therefore they could build huts. They had vegetation. Therefore they had materials to make huts. They had houses, shelter and stores.'

A system was devised for analysing group discussions and recording points made using this scale by dividing a page horizontally into 10 sections, recording synopses of points under levels and mapping the children's development of each other's arguments (Diagram 6.2). This analysis could then be transferred to a variety of other diagrammatic forms (Diagrams 6.3 and 6.4).

The story-writing test was assessed using a scale based on Ashby and Lee (1987) and Piaget (1932). This ranged from no awareness of ideas, beliefs and values and so no attempt to explain them, through intermediate levels when children mention symbolic artefacts in passing, but do not reflect on the ideas they may represent, and finally to an attempt to suggest the significance of symbols.

THE FINDINGS

The relationship between interpreting evidence and the development of historical imagination and empathy – implications for story-writing

In analysing the written 'evidence tests' unit 1, The Stone Age, it became apparent that the deductive reasoning scale reflected levels of argument, but did not reflect a difference in the quality of the answers of the control and experimental groups. The experimental groups' answers were more varied and more closely derived from the evidence, while the control group often simply repeated given information which was not rooted in the evidence. The control group displayed more anachronisms, and stereotypes and the assumption that people in the past were simple. Given a plan of a stone circle, for example, the experimental children suggested a variety of possible purposes (KM 'reconed it was for war dances, trading flint, praying'), and they suggested how it may have been made. The control group answers were dominated by repeating received information about 'magic oak trees', 'Druids in white cloaks', and 'scarey magic'.

This difference in quality was examined further in unit 2. Answers were grouped under Collingwood's (1939) three categories of historical enquiry: How was it made? How was it used? What did it mean to people at the time? The following analysis of the experimental groups' responses to the 'Waterloo Helmet' evidence (British Museum slide) shows how they considered each of these questions (although they had not been explicitly asked to do so). They had been asked 'what do you know for certain? What reasonable guesses can you make, and what would you like to know?'. Their answers suggest that it is through asking questions of evidence that children gradually learn to consider and attempt to explain the viewpoints of people who lived in other times. It also seems likely that the experimental groups were better able to do this because they had been taught through discursive teaching strategies which encouraged them to make a range of valid suppositions about evidence.

Experimental groups

Written test

Discussion tapes

I How Was it Made?

HC Exp 1. Qu I NVR 97
'They had metals…they could make things.'

JG Exp 2. Qu I NVR 120
'They could smelt iron and bronze…they had a furnace for getting iron out of rock

IW Exp 1. Qu I NVR 123
'They had charcoal to sep-arate metal from ore.'

ML Exp 1. Qu 3 NVR 102
'I would like to know if the horns were hollow, because if they are it would be lighter.'

RL Exp 1. Qu I NVR 107

JH Exp 2. NVR 100
'They made it carefully with the right kind of metals. Certainly they used a mould and little rivets.'

MF Exp 2. NVR 129
'They had the right tools to shape the metal.'

NH Exp 1. NVR 105
'They could print patterns on it. They had a habit of putting circles on their working.'

GP Exp 1. NVR 133
'They had weapons – shields and swords too. At the British Museum,

'They must have had good minds to remember things
.... They knew how to get to learn.'

I copied a sword with a bronze hilt.'

II What was it used for?

(a) For protection in battle

HG Exp 1. Qu 2 NVR 129
'They wore it to protect their heads...they had fights. They made it...they made weapons. They had wars.'

NH Exp 1. NVR 105
'They invented things. They knew how to smelt metal.'
Exp 1.
'It's got horns. It looks fierce – like an ox that could kill. Like a Stone-Age hunter's deer antlers – to hide in the bushes. The pattern could show what side you were on so you didn't kill your own men.'
'They fought for food. If there was a bad winter and cattle died... to steal an other tribe's cattle, or to cut another tribe's corn if they didn't have enough.'

MF Exp 2. Qu 3 NVR 129
'I would like to know how they got the idea of armour, and why did they fight?'

(b) As a ceremonial symbol or trophy

KC Exp 2. Qu 2 NVR 111
'It might be made for a chief... he would wear it at ceremonies to look special.'

NH Exp 1. NVR 105
'Maybe the more metal you had it showed how high up you were. They'd start with a bracelet 'til they were all covered in metal then they'd be a chief.'

NH Exp 1. Qu 2 NVR 105
'They might have used it at chariot races... they might have had it as a medal. They might have liked beautiful things and had it as an ornament.'

Exp 2.
'It may have been awarded for extreme bravery in battle. Or in a contest for new warriors. Maybe they had races and contests, and the armour was awarded for use in a battle.'

SH Exp 1. Qu 2 NVR 104
'It might have been for a goddess.'

Exp 1.
'If they found other things in the River Thames, they may be offerings to a water goddess, to

(c) A commodity to trade

ES   Exp 1. Qu 3 NVR 129
'How did the archaeologists come to find it, because it would tell me if it was made there, or if they traded them.'

RL   Exp 1. Qu 3 NVR 107
'And was there one people in the place who made them?... if he did he would be rich.'

II   What did it mean to the people who wore it?

PC   Exp 2. Qu I NVR 114
'They were not afraid of going into battle...they looked fierce...they put fierce patterns on them.'

ML   Exp 1. Qu 2 NVR 102
'I guess it had a kind of strap.'

KL   Exp 1. Qu 3 NVR 107
'Did they make different shapes and sizes, because it would have to fit... ?'

DS   Exp 1. Qu 3 NVR 88
'I would like to know what it felt like to put it on. It must have been heavy to handle. '

thank her for water to drink.'

Exp 2.
'They could have traded it for helmets made in another land. Or maybe for metal to make more weapons. Maybe, as we learned in a lesson, Julius Caesar wrote they used rods of equal weight, or coins, to trade. They could have traded it for bronze or iron - probably for metal of some kind.'

Exp 2.
'The patterns make it look sort of mysterious – they look like flowers... it might mean something like "long live our tribe" or "our tribe is the horse tribe". Or special orders from their God. Or a magic helmet to help them in battle. Or the wearer's name. Or to describe the wearer – how good he was at hunting or fighting.'

Exp 2.
'The strips at the side probably had vines or strings attached to hold it on to the wearer... they must have put something on it to make it shine... maybe it was measure for the wearer's head.'

Exp 1.
'It's so heavy they probably took it with them and put it on when they got there.'

When the study was planned, it had seemed that making deductions from evidence and historical imagination were different and discrete aspects of historical thinking, and for this reason, separate evidence and story-writing tests were devised. However, analysis of the evidence tests suggested that historical imagination develops through making valid suppositions about how things were made and used in the past and so considering what they may have meant to people at the time, and that this is the vehicle through which historical empathy may develop. Since historical imagination and historical empathy are defined in innumerable ways, their relationship as defined in this study is given in Diagram 6.1.

This has implications for story-writing in history. Analysis of the story-writing tests showed that while children enjoy trying to reconstruct the past through story-writing, and that they do consider and try to explain ideas and beliefs different from their own, their knowledge is limited and they are immature so that they are unable to take a holistic view of society (Furth, 1980). In writing stories, imagination is not necessarily tied closely to evidence, and interpretations of evidence do not have to be argued as they do in discussion. Therefore, anachronisms and misunderstandings are more likely to go unchecked. (Historical fiction is very difficult to write.) In the Stone Age unit, for example, the children were given a postcard of the Barnack Grave, 1800 BC (BM PR 34) with drawings of the grave goods, a walrus or whale-bone pendant,

Diagram 6.1: *Relationship between historical imagination and historical empathy as defined in this study*

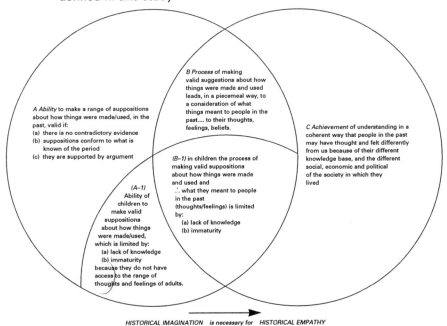

A *Ability* to make a range of suppositions about how things were made/used, in the past, valid if:
(a) there is no contradictory evidence
(b) suppositions conform to what is known of the period
(c) they are supported by argument

B *Process* of making valid suggestions about how things were made and used leads, in a piecemeal way, to a consideration of what things meant to people in the past.... to their thoughts, feelings, beliefs.

C *Achievement* of understanding in a coherent way that people in the past may have thought and felt differently from us because of their different knowledge base, and the different social, economic and political of the society in which they lived

(B–1) in children the process of making valid suppositions about how things were made and used and ∴ what they meant to people in the past (thoughts/feelings) is limited by:
(a) lack of knowledge
(b) immaturity

(A–1) Ability of children to make valid suppositions about how things were made/used, which is limited by:
(a) lack of knowledge
(b) immaturity
because they do not have access to the range of thoughts and feelings of adults.

HISTORICAL IMAGINATION   is necessary for   HISTORICAL EMPATHY a bronze dagger, a wristguard and a decorated pot, and asked to write a story called 'The Death of the Archer'. About one third of the children explained this with a story which attached no significance to the grave goods. 'An archer was doing pottery. He might have been shaping it with a dagger. The spear was to protect him. Someone came to the door and threw a flint at him and he fell on the fire.' Others may regard the objects as significant, but they did not reflect on why. Children are caught in a time-warp and see the archer die. 'They bury him with all his things, a bone necklace, a bronze dagger and a large pot,' or the archer was killed in a battle. 'His wife put some of his things around the fire before they burned him. '

At the highest level of response to emerge stories contained more detailed description of artefacts and more complicated narrative: 'In a village there lived a boy called Balloo. He was learning to do archery. Every three weeks he would get a feather. One day he was given a brilliant surprise – a wristguard; the chance to be a hunter with all the others. . .'. However there was no attempt to explain the significance of the grave goods or the ideas they represented.

It is not suggested that children should never be asked to write stories about the past, but 'Imagine you were. . .' should be treated with caution. If they are asked to do this, children need to be shown how to relate a reconstruction to evidence. Sylvester (1989) showed how a seven-year-old can use knowledge based on evidence from a pictorial source to write a story about the bubonic plague and the fire, and how a 12-year-old can use directories, plans and logs to write about a day in the life of a Victorian boy. Little (1989) gives two examples of story-writing by 10-year-olds about Spain's conquest of the Inca. In one, a different way of life, hierarchy and ceremony are understood and factual information has been translated into a reconstruction, while in the other, knowledge is thrown in without a sense of time or detail.

Assessing levels of argument

The written evidence tests

In the written evidence tests, the children were given an answer paper which they were told to fill in, pretending they were archaeologists reporting on the evidence (the example shows how Andrew filled in his 'archaeologist's' report on the petroglyphics at the end of the Stone Age unit). Answer papers were laid out to encourage the highest levels of response, based on the 10 point scale described on p. 118. They made a distinction between 'knowing', 'guessing', and 'not knowing', and encouraged children to make two statements for each of these categories, to follow each with a sequential argument and to write a 'conclusion'.

However, it was frequently necessary to look for the underlying logic of the thinking processes behind an answer in order to assess the level of thinking. Often this was obscured by poor spelling or handwriting. An answer may span several levels and would then be scored on the basis of the highest scoring statements within the answer and lower levels ignored. The logic of the answer does not always correspond to the divisions on the paper, so that the statements need to be carefully considered.

The oral evidence tests

Diagram 6.2 shows how the oral evidence tests were also analysed on the 10 point scale.These synopses refer to the written evidence used in the Iron Age unit (Strabo 1.4.2).

> Most of the island is level and well-wooded, but there are many hilly districts. It produces corn, cattle, gold, silver and iron. They are all exported, together with leather, slaves and good hunting dogs. The Gauls use these dogs, and their own, for war as well.

Diagram 6.3 shows how the levels were then mapped, so that they could be transferred to tables, to compare levels of argument achieved in individual written answers and in group discussion, over the four periods of study.

Making a distinction between 'knowing' and 'supposing'

In the written 'evidence tests' the children were asked three questions about each piece of evidence: question one, what do you know for certain? question two, what reasonable 'guesses' can you make? question three, what would you like to know? It is interesting that they were able to make these distinctions. Analysis of the unled discussion tapes, where they were not specifically asked to differentiate between knowing, guessing and not knowing, nevertheless show the discussions dominated by probability words (could be, maybe, unlikely, I wonder, what you think?). The children occasionally make certainty statements. 'They (the axe heads), were all chipped and smoothed' and sometimes these are challenged by other children: 'It's got two heads.' (cave painting). 'That could be a tail.' 'Bit thick for a tail.'

The unled groups also sometimes mention things that they would like to know. 'It must have been for some reason?' 'How do you think they made the banks?'

It is interesting that in the written 'evidence tests' the children were able to make 'certainty' statements, and reasonable guesses (questions 1 and 2) with almost equal ease. The graph (Figure 6.1) based on analysis of variance tests to compare groups, questions and types of evidence in each unit, shows a significant difference between the types of question, with question 3 (what would you like to know?), by far the most difficult. The Sheffe test of multiple

126

NAME _Andrew_ DATE 6,12.85

UNIT ONE THE STONE AGES

EVIDENCE Writing

What do you know FOR CERTAIN from this evidence?   Level 9

	Therefore	**Conclusion**
they communicated	they made signs for communicating	they needed other people
they draw	**Therefore** They had thing to draw with	

What reasonable GUESSES can you make about it?   Level 8

	Therefore	**Conclusion**
they may of had spcshells thing to do writing with		they might of had Spcsbell hunting Signs
I think it had a meaning	**Therefore** It migh of taken them a long time to get the writing	

What would you LIKE TO KNOW about it?   Level 6

	Because	**Conclusion**
What it ment	then we could make little word	
had they got to know wHat the signs ment	**Because** then we could do stone age writing.	

Diagram 6.2: *Synopsis of led and unled discussion showing how it is represented as a diagram*

Unit 2 Test 5 led discussion experimental group 1: JW, JB, GP, MS, BK, CB. T=Teacher

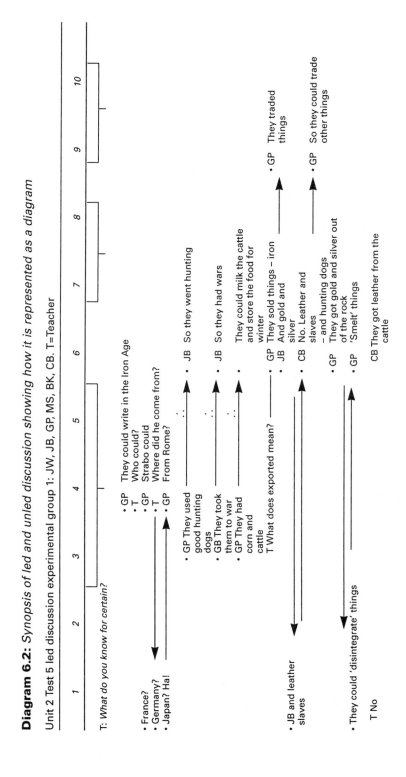

Diagram 6.2: *Cont*

Unit 2 Test 5 led discussion

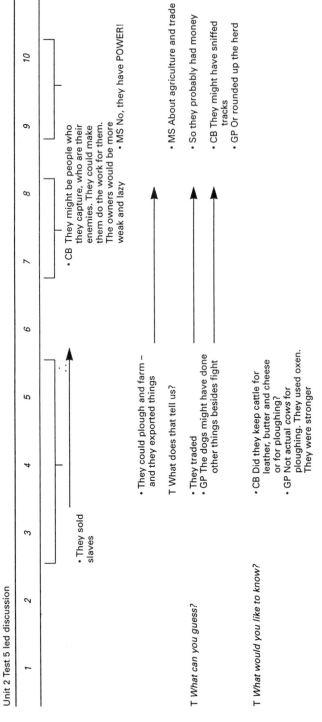

1   2   3   4   5   6   7   8   9   10

• They sold slaves

• CB They might be people who they capture, who are their enemies. They could make them do the work for them. The owners would be more weak and lazy   • MS No, they have POWER!

• They could plough and farm – and they exported things

T *What does that tell us?*

• They traded
• GP The dogs might have done other things besides fight

• MS About agriculture and trade

• So they probably had money
• CB They might have sniffed tracks
• GP Or rounded up the herd

T *What can you guess?*

T *What would you like to know?*

• CB Did they keep cattle for leather, butter and cheese or for ploughing?
• GP Not actual *cows* for ploughing. They used oxen. They were stronger

T *Is there anything else you would like to know?*   Unanimous 'no!'

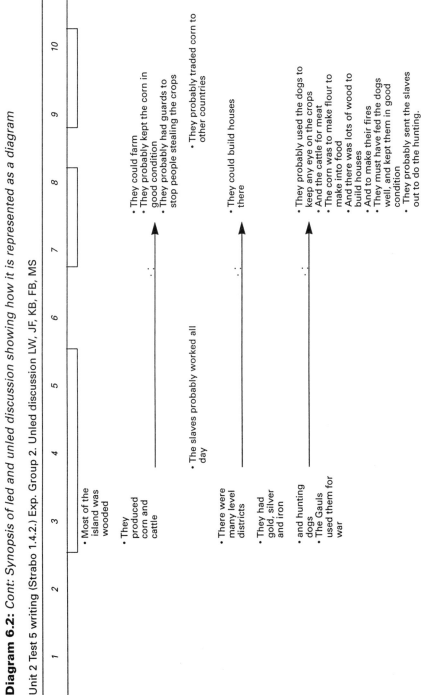

Diagram 6.2: *Cont: Synopsis of led and unled discussion showing how it is represented as a diagram*

Unit 2 Test 5 writing (Strabo 1.4.2.) Exp. Group 2. Unled discussion LW, JF, KB, FB, MS

1	2	3	4	5	6	7	8	9	10

• Most of the island was wooded

• They produced corn and cattle

    • They could farm
    • They probably kept the corn in good condition
    • They probably had guards to stop people stealing the crops

          • They probably traded corn to other countries

• The slaves probably worked all day

• There were many level districts

    • They could build houses there

• They had gold, silver and iron

• and hunting dogs
• The Gauls used them for war

    • They probably used the dogs to keep any eye on the crops
    • And the cattle for meat
    • The corn was to make flour to make into food
    • And there was lots of wood to build houses
    • And to make their fires
    • They must have fed the dogs well, and kept them in good condition
    • They probably sent the slaves out to do the hunting.

Diagram 6.3: *Led and unled discussions*
Unit 2, Test 5, writing. Strabo (1.4.2.)

	Exp. Group 1 Led Discussion				Exp. Group 2 Unled Discussion			
Level	1/2	3/4/5	7/8	9/10	1/2	3/4/5	7/8	9/10

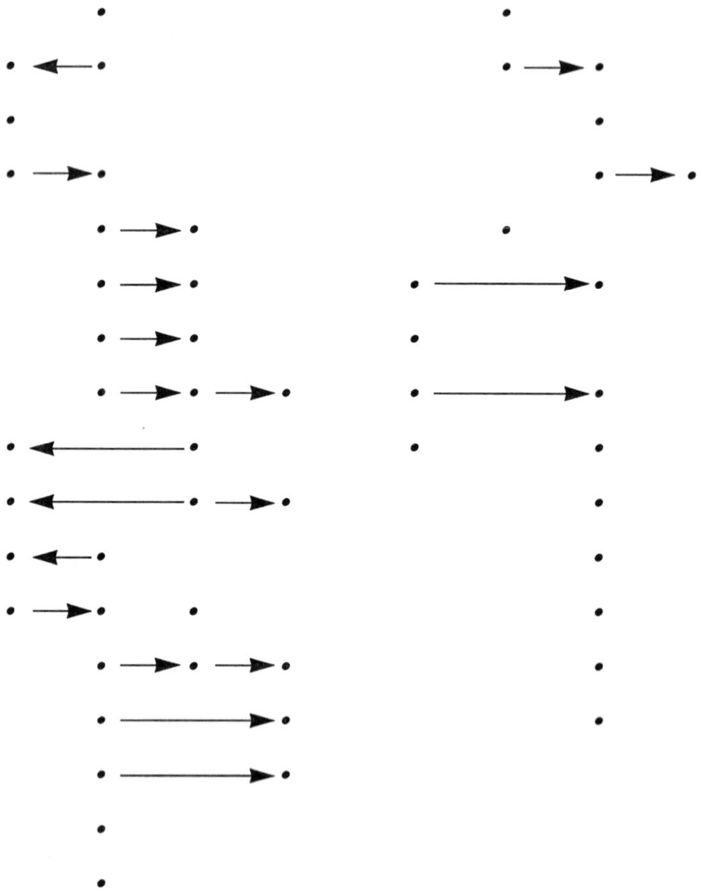

Points made at each level in led and unled discussions

Led Discussion		Unled Discussion	
level 1/2	5 points	level 1/2	4 points
level 3/4/5	13 points	level 3/4/5	3 points
level 7/8	8 points	level 7/8	11 points
level 9/10	5 points	level 9/10	1 point
Total:	31 points	Total:	19 points

Figure 6.1: *Graph showing means of scores for questions 1, 2 and 3 for units 1, 2 and 4* (Unit 3 was taught and tested, but the results were not analysed due to shortage of time.) The marking scale is outlined on p. 119.

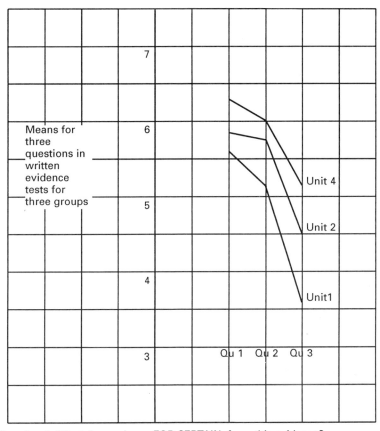

Question 1 What do you know FOR CERTAIN, from this evidence?
Question 2 What REASONABLE GUESSES can you make from this evidence?
Question 3 What WOULD YOU LIKE TO KNOW about this evidence?

comparison shows the difference between the first two questions and question 3 to be significant. These children then are able to make a distinction between knowing and valid suppositions, and they find both types of inference equally easy, but they find it far harder to say what they 'would like to know' about evidence.

Although these results were statistically significant, there were exceptions to the main effects. There were significant interactions between the questions and types of evidence. In unit I, for example, there was little difference in difficulty between knowing and guessing about the cave painting, the plan of the stone circle, or the map. This is not surprising because not much is known about how these things were made or used or what they meant to Stone Age people, even by archaeologists, so there are fertile opportunities for reasonable guesses. On the other hand, it was easier to make certainty statements about axe-heads because these are central to a study of the Stone Age. The experimental groups had three lessons on tools and weapons and had seen them made at Grimes Graves. This is important because it shows how statistically significant main effects are blurred by other variables, by a particular example of a type of evidence, by interest and by motivation.

There do however, seem to be implications for teachers, in the general finding, that children are equally able to say what they know, and to make reasonable suggestions, but find it difficult to say what they 'would like to know'. It suggests that children of this age do not need to be restricted to repeating 'facts' and that they are able to become actively involved in historical problem-solving. They can learn to control their own thinking, and become increasingly aware of what constitutes a valid supposition. This is an important staging post on the way to true historical understanding. However, 'what would you like to know?' is a question with an unknown starting point, and is too open. It does not encourage children to control their own investigation. This is significant because children are frequently told to 'find out about...', particularly at the ends of chapters in history books, assuming this encourages motivation and independent learning. These tests suggest that such a question is too unstructured.

Different types of evidence

The study set out to investigate whether children find it easier to make deductions about artefacts and pictures than about more abstract evidence, diagrams, maps and written sources. The relationship between groups, questions and evidence in each unit was statistically analysed using analyses of variance. The findings are shown in Figure 6.2.

Although in unit 1 there was a significant difference between the levels of response to the five types of evidence, and the children found the diagram and the map the most difficult, it is interesting that by unit 2, and again in unit 4, there was no significant difference in their ability to interpret 'concrete' and 'abstract' evidence. This is not to suggest that it is not very important for children to be introduced to artefacts and pictures (which are, at the very least, stimulating sources), but rather that if they are given more abstract evidence as well, as part of a continuum and have learned to discuss evidence, they can interpret abstract sources equally well. This seems to be because, having learned how to discuss evidence and the kinds of responses required, they can relate abstract evidence to 'concrete' evidence – maybe through visits to sites or museums. The experimental groups had visited Grimes Graves, the British Museum and local sites, and related these to maps, geology, vegetation and relief. They could therefore draw on these experiences in interpreting, for

Figure 6.2: *Graph showing means of scores for five types of evidence for units 1, 2 and 4* (Unit 3 was taught and tested, but the results were not analysed due to shortage of time.) The marking scale is outlined on p. 119.

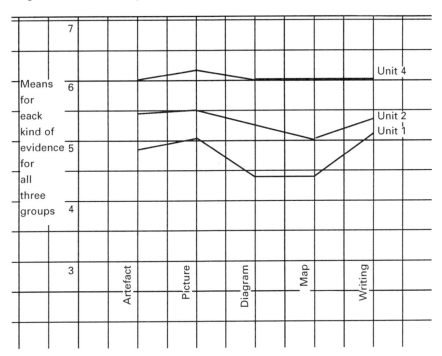

example, the Stone Age axe-heads, the Waterloo Helmet, the plans of the stone circle, the Iron Age hut, and the maps.

Their level of response depends, not on the level of abstraction of the evidence, but on language, on concepts and on argument, because remains of the past are only evidence to the extent that they can tell us about the people who made and used them. Children need to experience physical evidence, and to learn to discuss it, if it is to have meaning for them. They are then able to transfer this process to new evidence, and to more abstract evidence.

There are implications here for older students. It has often been assumed that artefacts and pictures are more appropriate for younger children who cannot read and write easily. However, if tangible sources are not easier to interpret, this strengthens the case for using a range of sources at any level of study.

Again, it is important to bear in mind that while the main effects shown in Figure 6.2 are statistically significant, there were variations in this pattern, influenced by particular examples of evidence, and by teaching strategies. In unit 4, the level main effect across the five kinds of evidence resulted from opposite trends across the experimental and control groups, although the span was only across one mark. It is likely that the control group found the Beowulf extract easier to interpret than the other evidence because they had more

134

Figure 6.3: *The taught concepts in unit 2 used in discussion tapes*

1 cm. represents the use of the concept in one evidence test on one or more occasions

■ represents led discussion groups (Exp 1)
▢ represents unled discussion groups (Exp 2)

Led (Exp 1)				*Unled* (Exp 2)	
Concrete	11			Concrete	9
Abstract	9			Abstract	8
Superordinate	10			Superordinate	1

This bar chart shows how both the led and unled groups used their taught vocabulary in unit 2 discussions and, when appropriate, used concepts learned in unit 1. The led groups, however, used more superordinates than the unled groups

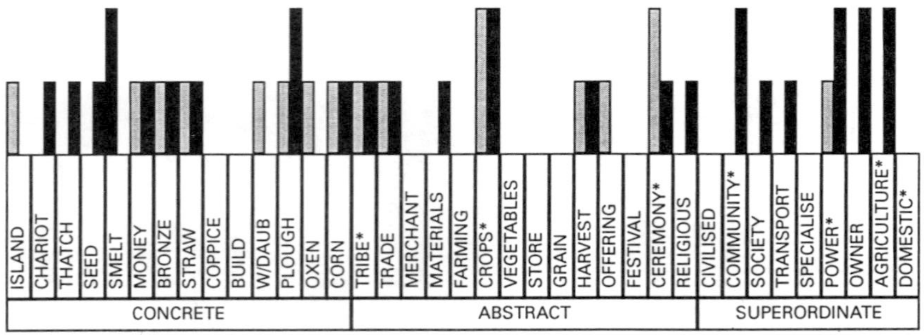

Note: * concepts learned in unit 1.

Figure 6.4: *Concepts taught in unit 1 or unit 2 which were used in written evidence tests in unit 4 by Exp 1, Exp 2 and control group children*

This bar chart shows how children in both experimental groups retained concepts learned in units 1 and 2 and applied them in their answers to unit 4. The control group used no abstract key concepts

Concrete		Abstract		Superordinate	
Exp 1	9	Exp1	34	Exp 1	15
Exp 2	11	Exp 2	29	Exp 2	5
C	2	C	2	C	0

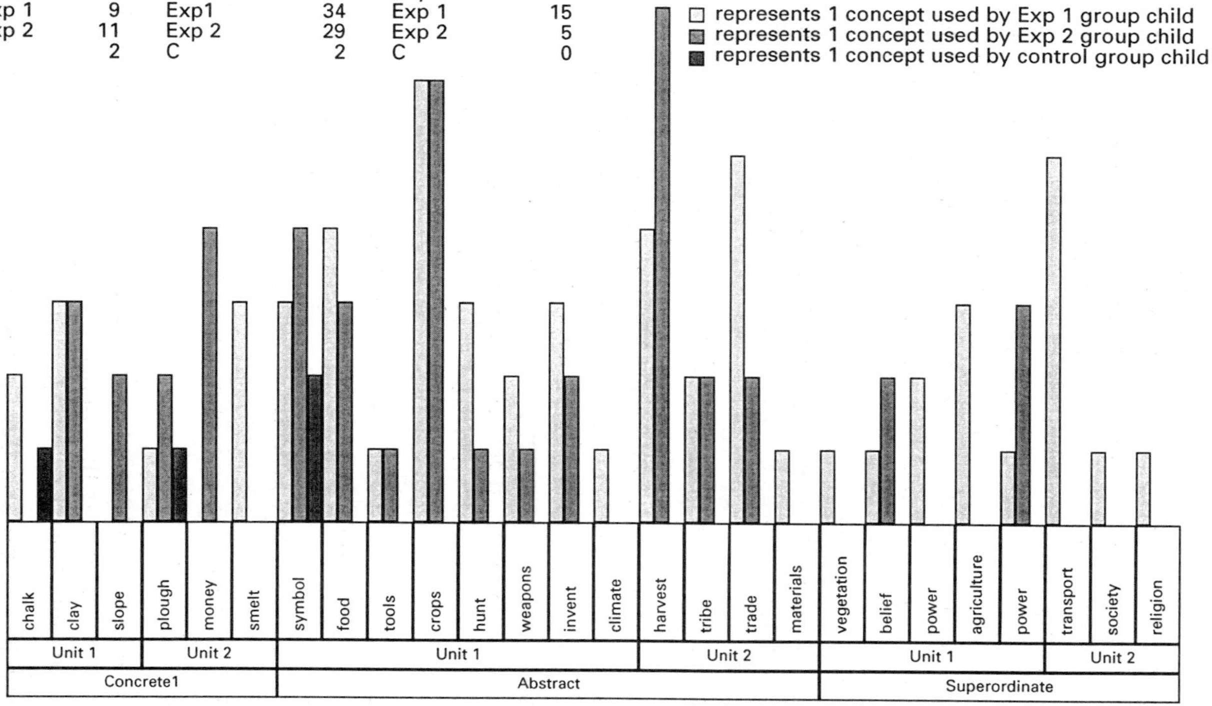

□ represents 1 concept used by Exp 1 group child
▨ represents 1 concept used by Exp 2 group child
■ represents 1 concept used by control group child

experience of 'comprehension exercises' but they had not learned how to interpret historical evidence.

Using learned concepts

The concepts which children had been taught in each unit as 'spellings' and which they had learned to use in discussing key evidence during class lessons the following week were used spontaneously by at least some of the children in both the written tests and the taped discussions. It was also encouraging that in unit 4, they were using vocabulary which they had learned in connection with previous units, transferring it to a new period and new material. Not surprisingly, the children in the control group who had not learned specific concepts only used those which were labelled in the evidence, and these were rarely abstract concepts. Figure 6.3 and Figure 6.4 show how children used concepts they had learned in previous units in both written and oral evidence tests.

Although no claim is made that the children totally understood the abstract concepts they used (e.g. vegetation, belief, power, agriculture, transport, society, religion), it seems that these concepts are becoming part of their own vocabulary.

It may be that the experimental groups were able to make a far greater range of valid suppositions about the evidence because they had a conceptual framework of both concrete and abstract concepts to which they could relate new pieces of evidence, even if the concepts themselves were not mentioned in their answers. Freedman and Loftus (1971) concluded that concepts play an important part in organising semantic memory. For example, in interpreting the written evidence in the Iron Age unit (see p. 144) many children make deductions concerned with trade, agriculture, metal production and social structure.

IW 'We know that Grece people traded with us. . .they must have had something to trade with.'

FF 'We know that gold, silver and iron are all exported across the see. '

NH They had corn and cattle. . .they could farm and so they had learned to live in one place. . .'

MF guessed that 'since they had gold, silver and iron, they had miners' and he wondered how they mined and transported it because he had seen neither mining tools nor Iron Age boats in pictures.

Similarly, in interpreting the illuminated Saxon manuscript showing harvest, children in the experimental groups focused on ideas connected with agriculture, community, and communication. They discussed crops, farming methods and the cycle of the farming year.

> RD 'The people seem to be cutting logs and transporting them maybe to trade them – if they lived near a forest.'

They refer to the jobs people are doing and the relationship between them, and make various suggestions about the meaning of the writing.

It seems then that not only do children enjoy learning to use and spell 'hard words', but that learning key concepts gives them a reference point, or framework, to apply to new material, and that this helps to generate a range of new ideas about it.

Led and unled group discussion

The content of the discussion was similar in both the led and unled groups. It was concerned with how the evidence may have been used and what it may have meant to those who created it, although the children had not been asked at any point to consider these aspects. However, the groups differed in the way they expressed their ideas. The led groups tended to make general statements and seemed to assume that the teacher knew where the discussion was leading, whereas the unled groups paid more attention to physical description, and sometimes explained their ideas through valid stories and images, about brave warriors for example, who may be commemorated by a stone circle, or who may have hidden their treasure there and defended it. However, in both the led and unled groups, there was genuine argument. They both made some illogical points. In the unled groups, they were either ignored or corrected, with respect, by another child. In the led groups, it was usually the teacher who queried them. In both groups, the children developed each other's points and the quality of the discussion improved over the four units.There was an increase in the numbers of points made and in the number of sequential arguments, and a decrease in the number of illogical points. The structure of the discussions differed slightly in the led and unled groups. The led groups tended to explore all the possibilities suggested by one point, then move on to the next point whereas the unled groups usually followed up a point with one further argument, then made a fresh point. Sometimes, they back-tracked, and ideas were less systematically explored.

It seems then that both led and unled discussions have a place in helping children to interpret evidence. If children have learned the thinking patterns required, discussion in small groups without the teacher may sometimes be more valuable than teacher-led discussion; children are more able to explain their ideas in their own way, to defend them and so to make them their own. This has implications for classroom organisation and for the value of group work not directly led by the teacher.

Diagram 6.4: *A comparison of the content of the led and unled discussions about previously unseen evidence. Unit 4. The Saxons*

Led Discussion   Unled Discussion

Test 1. Artefact. The Sutton Hoo Sceptre

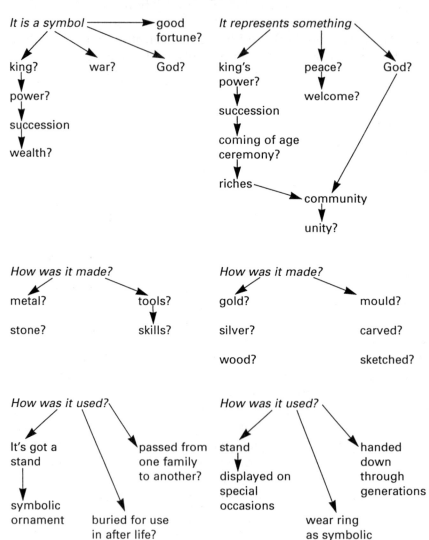

Diagram 6.4: *Cont.*

Led Discussion   Unled Discussion

Test 2. Illuminated Picture of Harvest from Saxon Calendar

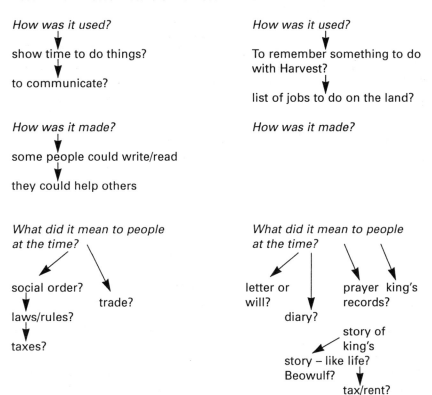

How was it used?
↓
show time to do things?
↓
to communicate?

How was it made?
↓
some people could write/read
↓
they could help others

*What did it mean to people
at the time?*
social order?   trade?
↓
laws/rules?
↓
taxes?

How was it used?
↓
To remember something to do
with Harvest?
↓
list of jobs to do on the land?

How was it made?

*What did it mean to people
at the time?*
letter or   prayer king's
will?   records?
↓
diary?
story of
king's
story – like life?
Beowulf?   ↓
tax/rent?

Test 3. Diagram. Plan of Saxon Church at Cirencester

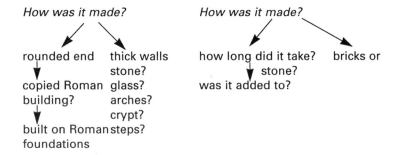

How was it made?
rounded end   thick walls
↓   stone?
copied Roman glass?
building?   arches?
↓   crypt?
built on Roman steps?
foundations

How was it made?
how long did it take?   bricks or
↓   stone?
was it added to?

Diagram 6.4: *Cont.*

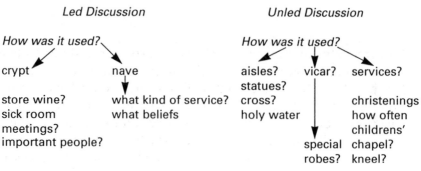

Led Discussion

How was it used?

crypt   nave

store wine?   what kind of service?
sick room   what beliefs
meetings?
important people?

Unled Discussion

How was it used?

aisles?   vicar?   services?
statues?
cross?   christenings
holy water   how often
          childrens'
special   chapel?
robes?   kneel?

Test 4. Map of the Croydon Area in Saxon Times

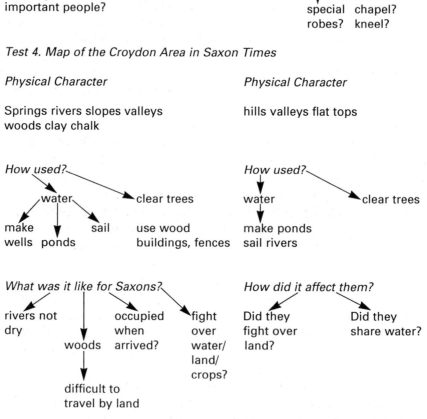

Physical Character

Springs rivers slopes valleys
woods clay chalk

Physical Character

hills valleys flat tops

How used?

water   clear trees

make   sail   use wood
wells   ponds   buildings, fences

How used?

water   clear trees

make ponds
sail rivers

What was it like for Saxons?

rivers not   occupied   fight
dry   when   over
     woods   arrived?   water/
                 land/
                 crops?
difficult to
travel by land

How did it affect them?

Did they   Did they
fight over   share water?
land?

Teaching strategies

Visits

The children were able to transfer information learned on visiting a site to new evidence. For example, on the visit to Farthing Down, they had been asked how, if they had lived there in Neolithic times, they could have made a dry, warm, comfortable shelter, what they could have eaten, where they might have found water, how they might have made tools, weapons and pots. When given a map of another similar area of the North Downs they were able to apply these points to the new map and make a range of deductions and suggestions in their written answers. Table 6.2 shows the information children had discussed on their visit to Farthing Down on the left. This visit stimulated their deductions about the map of a similar but unknown area which are given on the right.

The scores were surprisingly high for such abstract evidence; this seems to be because the visit enabled the children to relate real experiences and images to the map. As AW wrote in his conclusion 'This is the *best* evidence game'!

Similarly, in the Iron Age unit, they had again visited Farthing Down to trace the lynchets, the soil banks formed by turning the plough, which indicate Iron Age field patterns. Figure 6.5 shows how they were able to transfer discussion of these to the Iron Age map fields at Butser, on the South Downs.

At the end of unit 2 the children were given a previously unseen map of Iron Age fields on Butser Hill in Hampshire. In their written answers, experimental group 2 developed between them many of the arguments inherent in this evidence, which showed lynchets and trackways.

Table 6.3 analyses how children in the written answers related the new evidence about Butser to their visit to Farthing Down, and also to their class discussion on Iron Age farming, and finally to their own ideas. This shows how they were able to transfer the experience of the visit and following class discussion to new evidence, and, in doing so, also to form their own valid suggestions and questions.

The visits probably also helped them to discuss the plans of a stone circle, an Iron Age hut, and a Saxon church, although they had not visited similar sites, because they had considered geology, vegetation and relief, and the effects of these on a settlement in each period.

The stimulus of the 'further afield' visit to Grimes Graves and the British Museum probably helped the experimental groups to make a greater range of suppositions than the control group about artefacts, about the Stone-Age axe-heads, for example, and the Waterloo Helmet.

Table 6.2: *Examples of written answers, showing how visit to Farthing Down helped children to interpret the map*

Evidence discussed on visit to Farthing Down	Children's use of this evidence applied to the map (Exp Group A) Written Evidence
Geology: Top of Down is chalk with flints. Sparse vegetation and well-drained.	CL Qu 1. They had a lot of chalk. They could build huts on it because it's flat. They would not build a hut at the bottom of the hill because the water would not run away. (Score level 8) AM Qu 2. They would have camped on the slopes because when it rained the rain would run down the slope, their camp would not be flooded and their huts would not get destroyed. (Score level 7) CL Qu 3. I would like to know what flint implements were used for because they already had hand tools for killing animals. (Score level 6).
Clay soil – sticky – heavy	HC It has got a lot of clay on the surfis ... it must of been soggy. It must of been wet. (Score level 7) IW Qu 2. I can guess that they made things ... they would use clay to built pots. We can also guess that there is chalk ... there is flint. (Score level 8) HC Qu 2. There might have been a lot of wetness ... it could of been cold. There might of been stone age people living there ... they might of been living on the chalk bits.
In valley bottom there is marsh and a stream	ML Qu 2. They might have routes to the rivers ... they would have an easy way to go. They used pots to get water ... they can get water in time. (Score level 8).
Hachures show slopes	KM Qu 1. We know that Hachures mean steep slopes ... the hachures on the map mean there are shallow and steep slopes. (Score level 7).
Vegetation (+Geology) grass on top yew and oak on clay slopes	JW Qu 2. I can guess what kind of trees grew there ... I think oak and fir trees grew there. There were big chalk and clay areas where they could make pots. They could of lived near the clay area so they wouldn't have to walk far. (Score level 8) CL Qu 2. We can guess which plants they used for medicine ... some people knew which plants cure illnesses. We can also guess which plants and leaves they used for a bed ... they would choose the best things to make it. So they would select things to use. (Score level 7)
Animals	ES Qu 3. I would like to know if animals lived there when Stone Age lived because I want to see if they ate small animals.

Table 6.2: *Cont*

Evidence discussed on visit to Farthing Down	Children's use of this evidence applied to the map (Exp Group A) Written Evidence
	Examples. Experimental Group 2. Unit 1. Test 4. Showing use of visit in interpreting map
Geology: chalk/flint, clay, slope, wind, river	PC (level 8) Qu 1. They found that chalk sucks the water through it ... we know it was dry. They lived in places like Farthing Down. DF (level 9) Qu 2. They lived near to chalk and clay areas ... they didn't have to go far to get flints. They lived near slopes ... they were in a place with not many trees. They knew exactly where to live. JG (Level8) Qu 2. I guess they could have shelter from the cliffs ... they would be safe. They would have water ... they could have land for farming on the chalk soil. FB (level 8) Qu 2. They probably went fishing in the river ... they probably had quite a lot of fish. They probably had to wash in the river ... they probably didn't wash much! JG (level 8) Qu 1. Neolithic people must have been in the area ... they had camps there. Trees might be in great numbers on the clay soil ... they had shelter.
Vegetation	MF (level 7) Qu 3. Why they chose that place. What animals lived there, because I'd like to know what they ate. RF (level 7) Qu 2. I can guess there must have been a lot of woods ... I can guess there must have been lots of animals nearby. I know there
Animals	must have been a lot of food nearby.

Language: discussion, concepts and language as an objective tool

Discussion

Class lessons were based on discussion of selected evidence, using learned concepts. Each unit consisted of four such lessons taught over consecutive weeks. One of the four lessons was based on the local visit to an area of settlement, and one focused on ideas and beliefs.

This study endorsed the importance of learning through open-ended discussion, in which children learn the thinking processes of history. They learn that many suggestions are possible, and remain uncertain, and that arguments must be supported and can be contested. This is how criteria for validity become understood. It seems likely that this is the most important factor in the difference between the control group and experimental groups' responses. Firstly, the experimental groups achieved both a higher level of inferential reasoning, and a wider range of valid suppositions. Secondly, the control and

Figure 6.5: *How children were able to transfer their discussion of Iron Age field patterns seen on a visit to Farthing Down to a previously unseen map of field systems on Butser Hill, Hants.*

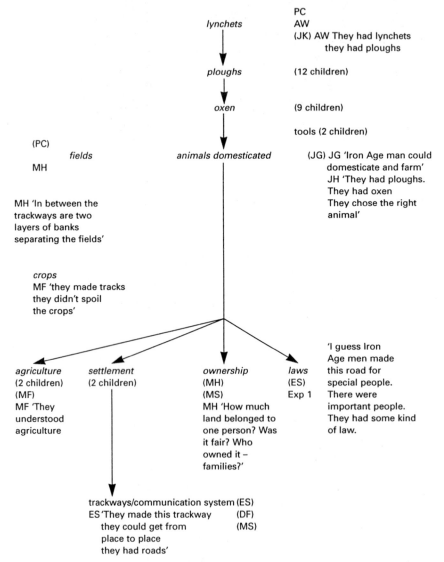

experimental groups used the factual information they had in different ways. They were not required to rehearse it in their answers but nevertheless, it underpinned their answers. The control group, however, tended to repeat information given, which was only loosely related to the evidence, and when they went beyond it, they often revealed misconceptions. The experimental groups were more likely to test given knowledge against the evidence. Their

Table 6.3

Butser Map	Farthing Down Visit	Class Discussion	Own Ideas
PC There are bumps. We know where the fields were	They could use machinery like a plough. They farmed. They grew crops.	There was probably a settlement there. They probably grew *vegetables* (re: evidence of beans, vetch, crop rotation)	If they thought a horse was a god or something why did they not use it? (in farming)
JG They had ploughs	They understood how to grow crops. They could farm and domesticate	There might be *tools* or there might be bones of oxen still there. (re: evidence of bones found, and tools, at Glastonbury) (re: oxen bones similar to modern Dexter)	A cart could carry crops from the field. How long did it take to make (invent?) a cart? If there are bones there, archaeologists could make up an oxen like they make dinosaurs in Natural History Museum
RF I know for certain this map give us clues. I know some people can find these ditches (i.e. I know they exist and what they look like)	I guess they had patterns in soil and chalk (i.e. I know soil or chalk is thin – viz the Uffington Horse	I guess they had *lambs* (re: sheep probably Soay, as at Butser) or as JK said 'sheep would give wool and meat and keep the grass down	
MS They had fields. They must have had a plough	I guess the tracks were for taking the plough across	They might grow things like peas and beans (re: Butser evidence)	I guess the tracks were made of wood. There must have been timber to make them from. I would like to know what transport they had, and we would know what skills they had

Table 6.3 *Cont*

Butser Map	Farthing Down Visit	Class Discussion	Own Ideas
SK They had roads	They could take the oxen across to another field because if the plough went over the corn it would crush it up and it would not grow again	I think had a field of *herbs* (re: discussion of flavouring and preserving)	They could eat them and (use them to) make other foods
MH In between the two trackways are the two layers of banks separating the fields	They must transport the plough through gaps in the banks	The blank bits might be for *settlements* (re: post hole evidence)	Maybe the owners might live there. Maybe ownership separated by trackways. I would like to know how much land belonged to one person; if they had the same amount and if they lived in families next to each other

suggestions, for example, about the Anglo-Saxon sceptre were dependent on their knowledge of Anglo-Saxon kings and kingdoms, laws and succession.

It seems, then, that discussion is important in the development of historical understanding. However the discussion must be based on selected key evidence. Children need key factual information, but if they learn it through discussion, they do not simply repeat it, but they both retain the information and are able to transfer the pattern of discursive thinking to new evidence.

Concepts

The importance of teaching and using selected concepts of different levels of abstraction to interpret key evidence has already been discussed (p. 150). It was seen that children were able to use abstract, learned concepts as an organising framework against which to test new evidence, even when they did not mention the concept itself. This helped them in discussing the Sutton Hoo sceptre to talk about the king, ceremonies, symbols and laws; Beowulf deductions involved power, vengeance, courage and beliefs. Learned concepts helped children to make a greater range of valid suggestions about evidence, to develop arguments, and so to make suggestions about different attitudes, behaviour and beliefs.

Language as an objective tool

The experimental groups had also discussed the nature of language as a tool for communication. They were able to talk about the relationship between the written and spoken word, the symbolism of language and to suppose how language originated and changed. A child could say of the Stone Age petroglyphics, for instance, 'They made signs for communicating; they had things to draw with; they needed people.' Or 'They wrote strange writing. . .they had different words from today. This writing is found in Italy. . .it could have been found in other place. . .'. One child wrote, 'They had to teach each other how to speak...they had to co-operate in making writing.' Another guessed that in different countries they had different signs. . .if someone went to a different country, he would not understand. It took a long time to carve the signs. . .they would not move from place to place.

In considering the Strabo excerpt in unit 2, JG wondered 'how long after the Romans the Iron Age wrote.' AW observed that 'they had different language over different times. They did not have the same language everywhere. . . I would like to know how they made their languages up. . .'

In unit 4, JG wondered, 'if the Saxons learned writing from the Romans,' but AW and DS guessed it was learned through the monks. 'I guess the monks wrote it. It would be in Latin.' 'Monks were taut to read and rit in neat ritting. . .' SH guessed that since they could write and were good at drawing, 'they probably had lituriture.' In interpreting the extract from Beowulf, children considered the significance of the language. 'I would like to know what Gaet means.' 'I would like to know why Grendel was called Grendel. It sounds strange. Is Grendel a Latin name or an English name?' 'I think that 'gable roof' is the bit just below the top of the house.' They also tried to explore the significance of writing in Saxon times. 'It is a Saxon poem. Therefore they had forms of writing. Beowulf was made up. Therefore it would be a folk tale or a legend. . .'

Acceleration

The study suggested that if children are taught consistently, applying the same teaching strategies to new material, they learn patterns of thinking which can be transferred, and the quality of their thinking improves. In unit 4, the experimental groups achieved higher levels of deductive argument than in previous units, and used more abstract concepts. It seems then that it is important for children to learn patterns of thinking, and for teachers to be clear what these should be. In unit 4, although the means for all three groups were higher than in the first two units, the means for the experimental groups were much higher than the control group mean (Figure 6.6).

The integrated curriculum

The study did not aim to prove the benefits of learning history through an integrated curriculum. However, the links between responses to the history tests and other areas of the curriculum can be traced. From the science components, the children seem to have learned both to question and respect the technology of other societies.

They discuss how things were made and used. For example, the discussion of the Waterloo Helmet reflects their knowledge of iron smelting learned in the Iron Age unit. Their experience of historical fiction (*The Changeling*, R. Sutcliffe; *The Dream Time and The Bronze Sword*, H. Treece) may well have helped children to recognise the difference between fact and imagination. There are many examples of children transferring their knowledge of geology, vegetation and relief to maps of other areas; geography probably also influenced their references to trade, transport, and migration of peoples. Art taught the experimental groups careful observation through drawing (slides of cave paintings, Iron Age artefacts in the British Museum, or AngloSaxon pottery). It also seems to have taught them both an interest in the techniques and materials used in the past, and an understanding and respect for different interpretations. SH guesses that 'Stone Age \people may have kept their oxides in pots and used their hands to paint. 'The experimental groups suggest why the Uffington Horse may be unrealistic. DS NVR 88 (Exp 1. Qu 1(7)) owns a horse and brings

Figure 6.6: *Graph showing means of evidence test scores for control and experimental groups for units 1, 2 and 4*

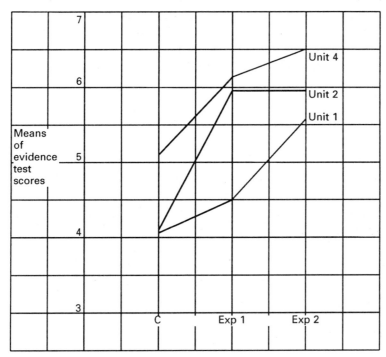

her own keen interest to bear, in spite of difficulties with spelling!

> I kown that they had Horse Because it is a piter of one. They must of copid the Bones of the Horse And the shape of the Horse And it must of bein bukin because of its back legs and the sape of it...

MH NVR 135 (Exp 2. Qu 1(9))

> Two of the legs do not join up to the body. Therefore I think that is a special 3D effect. It has whiskers on a kind of chin. Therefore either they have not observed well, or their horse has whiskers.

The dimension of religious education involved the discussion of the symbolism of light and dark in cave-painting and in other cultures, the needs and fears of Iron Age people, the nature of Roman Gods, the teachings of early Celtic and Roman missionaries. It may be that this helped children to consider reasons for beliefs and rituals in their own and other societies. The mathematics component may have encouraged deductions involving estimates. ('It might take 1000 people to fill the church. The population must have been big.') They consider shape. One child says of the circle, 'They had another shape in maths,' and the Uffington Horse has a 'special 3D effect'. The Iron Age fields are 'square or rectangular'.

An integrated project with a clear history focus seems the most economical way, in a crowded curriculum, to allow children to become steeped in a period. It also demonstrates that history involves the history of thought in all disciplines and in all aspects of society, and can, in turn, give a purpose to experiment in science and to calculations in mathematics.

WAYS IN WHICH TEACHERS CAN EVALUATE AND DEVELOP THE NATIONAL CURRICULUM IN THE LIGHT OF EXPERIENCE AND GOOD PRACTICE

This research indicates some of the problems involved in assessing patterns in the development of children's thinking in history. However, the study was undertaken as an integral part of class teaching, and refined the thinking of the teacher and the quality of her teaching in the process, so that it suggests that action research by practising teachers is both possible and desirable, and should therefore be supported and encouraged.

It is not necessary for such detailed analysis to be carried out all the time, or by all teachers; the purpose of the study described was to indicate broad patterns of development, and the relationship between different aspects of historical thinking which could form a basis for planning and for on-going assessment by teachers. It is essential that the broad brushstrokes with which the National Curriculum aims to paint a map of the past is also balanced by detailed and carefully focused discussion of key evidence. Young children cannot grasp a holistic view of complex social structures; they do not understand the workings of adult minds, and cannot address difficult political and religious issues. The need to list and memorise 'causes and effects' killed school history for many people and there is still a danger that teachers will over-interpret the content specified in the revised Curriculum.

Experience suggests that children are interested in detail, and in problem-solving in which they can be validly and genuinely engaged: what did sailors on the Armada ships eat? What did the sailors on the Mary Rose do? Who lived in my home before I did?

Therefore, the curriculum must be taught in an economical way if it is not to be overloaded. Planning must be carefully focused to centre on real problem-solving in each curriculum area, and in a range of contexts. Planning, activities and evaluation must form a related sequence so that assessment is an integral part of all the work children do and of the constant interaction between teacher and child. Work planned in history must reflect the thinking processes of history, and allow for a range of differentiated outcomes. It should also involve learning history through the rich variety of activities on which good primary practice is based:

- information technology (simulations, word-processing and datahandling);
- art (drawing, printing, painting, embroidery, model-making);
- science and technology (cooking, spinning, weaving, grinding seeds, building and testing structures, using tools, moving loads, using a range of materials);
- language for different audiences (transactional and expressive writing, reading, discussion, role-play, making video and audio tapes).

IN CONCLUSION

Teachers today face a different challenge from that encountered in 1991. In implementing the National Curriculum for history initially, they had to adjust to new ways of setting out and describing the curriculum. The prescription of content was new and the assessment requirements were cumbersome. Coming to terms with new ways of thinking was time-consuming and demanding. Now they are able to draw on experience gained since then; there were over 5,000 responses to the Dearing Review and these have shaped the revision.

Much remains that is familiar to teachers in the structure and terminology of the Revised Curriculum for history. There are also new, distinctive features. Only a minimum statutory framework remains. The planning is now soundly based on interaction between the content in each programme of study and the key elements running through each key stage which allow for progression in thinking. This is the basis for day-to-day setting of teaching objectives, formative assessment and feedback. The level descriptions which reflect the key elements are only intended to be used for summative assessment at the end of a key stage, based on work done in a number of contexts.

There are many opportunities to interpret the new framework for history in creative ways, planning activities which reflect an increased understanding of the nature of history, an articulate rationale for its importance, and the sharing of teachers' own enthusiasms. Nevertheless, the position of history in the curriculum is probably more precarious than before. The statutory requirement is minimal, with a recognition that some outline studies are inevitable; on the other hand, there is increasing emphasis on tests in 'basic skills' and on published league tables of the results. Yet

> The present is where we get lost
> If we forget our own past and have
> No vision of the future.

> (Ayi Kwei Arnah, in Fryer, 1989)

Whether or not this is allowed to happen will depend on the enthusiasm, efforts and expertise of all those who care about primary history, working together with conviction. This will involve convincing parents of the importance of history, if they are to understand, value and support it; involving them in visits and follow-up work, in collecting resources, organising school museums, collections, contributing to oral history, providing informed audiences for, or participating in presentations.

For this reason, one school always begins a term by inviting parents to a meeting at which work planned is explained: what the children will be doing, how and why.

A mother became sufficiently interested to watch a television programme about excavations at a Celtic hill fort which she talked about over breakfast the following morning with her eight-year-old son. 'But Mum', he asked, 'what is the *evidence* for that?' Another child, after a school visit to Canterbury Cathedral, took her grandparents on an informed investigation of their local cathedral in Norwich. If parents and guardians become involved in their children's work in history they understand the kinds of thinking this requires and can share in and respond to evaluations of topic books, presentations and models, so that summative, end of key stage assessment is meaningful and valued.

Professionals also need to support each other if history is to be seen as an important and valued part of the primary curriculum. Class teachers remain the key practitioners, but they are increasingly working with educators in museums and galleries, and in partnership with colleagues in higher education, to investigate new approaches through action research, as roles in teacher education change.

Education, like history, is a dynamic process and teachers are resilient and resourceful people who will surely respond – again – to the challenges ahead.

References

AMMA (1990) Proceedings of the Assistant Masters and Mistresses Association Address by Rt. Honourable John McGregor.

Andreetti, K. (1993) *Teaching History from Primary Evidence*. London: David Fulton.

Ashby, R. and Lee, P. J. (1987) 'Children's Concepts of Empathy and Understanding in History', in C. Portal (ed.) *The History Curriculum for Teachers*. Lewes: Falmer Press.

Ausubel, D. P. (1963) *The Psychology of Meaningful Verbal Learning*. Gruse.

Ausubel, D. P. (1968) *Educational Psychology. A Cognitive View*. London: Holt, Rinehart and Winston.

Barnes, D. and Todd, F. (1977) *Communication and Learning in Small Croups*. London: Routledge and Kegan Paul.

Batho, G. R. (ed.) (1994) *School Museums and Primary History*, Occasional Paper 7. London: The Historical Association.

Beard, R. M. (1960) 'The Nature and Development of Concepts', in *Educational Review* 13, No. 1, pp. 12–26.

Beattie, A. (1987) *History in Peril: May Parents Preserve It*. London: Centre for Policy Studies.

Beddoe, D. (1983) *Discovering Women's History*. London: Pandora.

Bernot, L. and Blancard, R. (1953) *Nouville, un Village Francis*. Paris: Institut d'Ethnologie.

Bersu, G. (1940) *Excavations at Little Woodbury* 6, pp.30–111.

Biott, C. (1984) Getting on Without the Teacher. Primary School Pupils in Cooperative Groups. Collaborative Research Paper 1. Sunderland Polytechnic. Schools Council Programme Two.

Blakeway, S. E. (1983) 'Some Aspects of the Historical Understanding of Children aged 7 to 11'. Unpub. MA Dissertation. London University Institute of Education.

Blyth, A. (1990) *Making the Grade for Primary Humanities*. Milton Keynes: Open University Press.

Blyth, J. E. (1982) *History in Primary Schools*. McGraw Hill. Open University Press (2nd edn, 1989).

Blyth, J. E. (1988) *History 5–9*. London: Hodder and Stoughton.

Blyth, J. (1994) *History 5 to 11*. London: Hodder and Stoughton.

Booth, M. B. (1969) *History Betrayed*. London: Longmans, Green and Co.

Booth, M. (1979) 'A Longitudinal Study of the Cognitive Skills, Concepts and Attitudes of Adolescents Studying a Modern World History Syllabus, and an Analysis of their Historical Thinking'. Unpub. PhD Thesis. University of

Reading.

Borke, H. (1978) 'Piaget's View of Social Interaction and the Theoretical Construct of Empathy', in L. E. Siegal and C. J. Brainerd (eds) *Alternatives to Piaget*. London: Academic Press.

Boulding, E. (1976) *Handbook of International Data on Women*. Beverley Hills: Sage.

Boulding, E. (1977) *Women in the Twentieth Century World*. New York: Sage.

Boulding, G. E. (1981) *The Underside of History*. Westview.

Bradley, N. C. (1947) 'The Growth of the Knowledge of Time in Children of School Age', in *British Journal of Psychology*, No. 38, pp. 67–8.

Bruner, J. S. (1963) *The Process of Education*. New York: Vintage Books.

Bruner, J. S. (1966) *Towards a Theory of Instruction*. The Belknap Press of Harvard U.P. (7th Ed, 1975).

Buck, M., Sally, I. and Moorse, K. (1994) *Educating the Whole Child: Cross-curricular Themes Within the History Curriculum*, Occasional Paper 10. London: The Historical Association.

Butterworth, G. and Light, P. (1982) (eds) *Social Cognition – Studies in the Development of Understanding*. Brighton: Harvester Press.

Clarke, R. R. (1960) *East Anglia*.

Collingwood, R. G. (1939) *An Autobiography* (pbk, 1970). London: Oxford University Press.

Coltham, J. (1960) 'Junior School Children's Understanding of Historical Terms'. Unpub. PhD Thesis. University of Manchester.

Cooper, H. J. (1991) 'Young Children's Thinking in History'. Unpub. PhD Thesis. London University Institute of Education.

Cooper, H. (1993) 'Removing the Scaffolding: A Case Study Investigating How Whole-class Teaching can lead to Effective Peer Group Discussion Without the Teacher' in *The Curriculum Journal*, Vol. 4, No. 3, pp. 385–401.

Cooper, H. (1994) in *Teaching History*, Ch. 5; Ch. 8. Hilary Bourdillon (ed.). London: Routledge.

Cooper, H. (1995) *History in the Early Years*. London: Routledge.

Cooper, H. (1996) 'Exploring Links between Whole Class Teaching and Small Group Discussion' in *TOPIC*, No. 15. Slough: National Foundation for Educational Research.

Cowie, E. E. (1985) *History and the Slow Learning Child*. Teaching History Series. H.A. No. 41.

Cox, M. V. (1986) *The Development of Cognition and Language*. Brighton: Harvester Press.

Crowther, E. (1982) 'Understanding of the Concept of Change among Children and Young Adolescents'. *Educational Review* 34, 3, pp.279–84.

Croydon and Stockport Workhouse. Community Information Resource Project (1989) Davidson Professional Centre. Croydon.

Da Silva, W. A. (1969) 'Concept Formation in History through Conceptual Clues'. Unpub. PhD Thesis. University of Birmingham.

Davis, J. (1986) *Artefacts in the Primary School*. Teaching History Series. No. 45, pp.6–8. The Historical Association.

DES (1978) 'Primary Education in England and Wales'. Survey by Her Majesty's Inspectors of Schools. London: HMSO.

DES (1982) *Education 5–9*. London: HMSO.

DES (1983) *9–13 Middle Schools: An Illustrative Survey*. London: HMSO.

DES (1986) *History in Primary and Secondary Schools*. London: HMSO.

DES (1989) *The Teaching and Learning of History and Geography*. London: HMSO.

DES (1991) *Inspection of Humanities Courses in Years 5–9 in 26 Schools*. London: HMSO.

DES (1991a) *History in the National Curriculum*. London: HMSO.

DES (1991b) *Starting with Quality. Report of the Committee of Enquiry into the Quality of Educational Experiences offered to 3- and 4-year-olds* (Rumbold Report). London: HMSO.

DFE (1995) *History in the National Curriculum*. London: HMSO.

Dick, R. (1992) *The Indus Valley Civilization: A Project for Key Stage 2*, a Young Historian Scheme Leaflet No. 4. London: The Historical Association.

Dickinson, A. K. and Lee, P. J. (1978) (eds) *History Teaching and Historical Understanding*. London: Heinemann.

Dickinson, A. and Lee, P. J. (1994) 'Investigating Progression in Children's Ideas about History: The CHATA Project' in *Partnership and Progress, New Developments in History Teacher Education and History Teaching*, pp. 78–101. USDE Papers in Education: University of Sheffield.

Doise, W., Mugny, C. and Perret Clermont, A. N. (1975) 'Social Interaction and the Development of Cognitive Operations', in *European Journal of Social Psychology* 5, pp.367–83.

Doise, W. (1978) *Groups and Individuals: Explanations in Social Psychology*. Cambridge: Cambridge University Press.

Doise, W. and Mugny, G. (1979) 'Individual and Collective Conflicts of Centrations in Cognitive Development', in *European Journal of Social Psychology* 9, pp. 105–9.

Donaldson, M. (1978) *Children's Minds*. London: Fontana.

Elton, G. R. (1970) 'What Sort of History Should we Teach?', in M. Ballard (ed.) *New Movements in the Study and Teaching of History*. Temple Smith.

Erikson, E. H. (1965) *Childhood and Society*. Harmondsworth: Penguin.

Famous Sailors (1970) Macdonald.

Ferguson, J., Montgomerie, D. and Price, M. (1995) *History – Studying the Facts, a National Curriculum Project for Key Stage 2 Linking History, Drama and English*, The Young Historian Scheme Leaflet No. 2. London: The Historical Association.

Flavell, J. H. (1985) *Cognitive Development* (2nd Edn). London and New York: Prentice Hall.

Fleming, K. (1992) 'A Land Fit for Heroes: Recreating the Past through Drama', in *Teaching History*, 68.

Freedman, J. L. and Loftus, E. F. (1971) 'Retrieval of Words from Long-Term Memory', in *Journal of Verbal Learning and Verbal Behaviour*, 10, pp. 107–15.

Friedman, K.C. (1978) 'Time Concepts of Elementary School Children', in *The Elementary School Journal*, No. 44, pp. 337–42.

Fryer, P. (1984) *Staying Power*. London: Pluto Press.

Fryer, P. (1989) *Black People in the British Empire – An Introduction*. London: Pluto Press.

Furth, H. G. (1980) The World of Grown Ups. New York: Elsevier.

Gagné, R. M. (1977) *The Conditions of Learning*. Rinehart and Winston.

Galton, M., Simon, B. and Croll, C. (1980) *Inside the Primary Classroom*. London: Routledge and Kegan Paul.

Garfield, L. and Blishen, E. (1970) *The God Beneath the Sea*. London: Longman.

Garvey, C. (1977) *Play*, The Developing Child Series. London: Collins/Fontana.

Getzels, J. W. and Jackson, P. W. (1962) *Creativity and Intelligence: Explorations with Students*. London and New York: Wiley.

Gittings, C. (1991) 'Portraits as Historical Evidence in the Primary School', in *Primary History Today*. Historical Association.

Goldstein, A. P. and Michels, G. Y. (1985) *Empathy: Developmental Training and Consequences*. Hillsdale N.J.: Lawrence Erlbaum Associates.

Green, J. (1992) *Native Peoples of the Americas*. Oxford: Oxford University Press

Guilford, J. P. (1959) 'Traits of Creativity' in H. H. Anderson (ed.) *Creativity and Its Cultivation*, pp. 142–61, Harper.

Haddon, F. A. and Lytton, H. (1968) 'Teaching Approach and the Development of Divergent Thinking Abilities in Primary Schools', in *British Journal of Educational Psychology*, Vol. 38, pp. 171–80.

Hallam, R.N. (1975) 'A Study of the Effect of Teaching Method on the Growth of Logical Thought, with Special Reference to the Teaching of History using Criteria from Piaget's Theory of Cognitive Development'. Unpub. PhD Thesis. University of Leeds.

Hamlyn, D. (1982) 'What Exactly is Social about the Origins of Understanding?' in G. Butterworth and P. Light (eds) *Social Cognition: Studies in the Development of Understanding*.

Harding, D. W. (1974) *The Iron Age in Lowland Britain*. London: Routledge and Kegan Paul.

Harner, L. (1982) 'Talking about the Past and the Future' in W. Friedman (ed.) *The Developmental Psychology of Time*. New York: Academic Press.

Harpin, W. (1976) *The Second 'R': Writing Development in the Junior School*. London: Allen and Unwin.

Hill, C. (1980) *The World Turned Upside Down: Radical Ideas during the English Revolution.* Harmondsworth: Penguin.

Hill, C. and Morris, J. (1991) *Practical Guides, History: Teaching Within the National Curriculum.* Leamington Spa: Scholastic Publications.

Historical Association (1987) 'History in the Core Curriculum'.

HMI Wales (1989) *History in the Primary Schools of Wales.* Welsh Office.

Hodgkinson, K. (1986) 'How Artefacts can Stimulate Historical Thinking in Young Children'. *Education 3–13,* Vol. 14, No. 2.

Horton, A. M. (1992) *Teaching the Aztecs: A Cross Curricular Perspective,* Bringing History to Life Series, No. 4. London: The Historical Association.

Hulton, M. (1989 'African Traditional Stories in the Classroom', in D. Atkinson (ed.) *The Children's Bookroom: Reading and the Use of Books.* Stoke on Trent: Trentham.

Huntley, E. L. (1993) *Two Lives, Florence Nightingale and Mary Seacole.* London: L'Ouverture Bogle.

Isaacs, S. (1948) *Intellectual Growth in Young Children.* London: Routledge and Kegan Paul.

Jahoda, G. (1963) 'Children's Concept of Time and History', in *Educational Review* 95.

Jones, R. M. (1968) *Fantasy and Feeling in Education.* London: London University Press.

Kitson Clarke, G. (1967) *The Critical Historian.* London: Heinemann.

Klausmeier, H. J. and Allen, P. S. (1978) *Cognitive Development of Children and Youth. A Longitudinal Study.* London: Academic Press.

Klausmeier, H. J. *et al.* (1979) *Cognitive Learning and Development.* Ballinger.

Knight, P. (1989a) 'Children's Understanding of People in the Past'. Unpub. PhD Thesis. University of Lancaster.

Knight, P. (1989b) 'Empathy: Concept, Confusion and Consequences in a National Curriculum', in *Oxford Review of Education* Vol. 15.

Knight, P. (1989c) 'A Study of Children's Understanding of People in the Past', in *Educational Review* Vol. 41, No. 3.

Knight, P. (1991) *History at Key Stage 1 and 2, A Practical Guide to Planning and Implementation.* London: Longman.

Knight, P. (1993) *Primary Geography, Primary History.* London: David Fulton.

Lawton, D. (1975) *Class, Culture and the Curriculum.* London: Routledge and Kegan Paul.

Leach, E. (1973) 'Some Anthropological Observations on Number, Time and Common Sense', in G. A. Howson (ed.) *Developments in Mathematical Education.* Cambridge: Cambridge University Press.

Lello, J. (1980) 'The Concept of Time, the Teaching of History and School Organisation', in *History Teacher.* Vol. 13, No. 3.

Light, P. (1983) in S. Meadows (ed.) *Developing Thinking Approaches to Children's*

Cognitive Development. London and New York: Methuen.

Light, P. (1986) 'The Social Concomitants of Role-Taking', in M. V. Cox *The Development of Cognition and Language.* Brighton: Harvester Press.

Little, V. (1989) 'Imagination and History' in J. Campbell and V. Little (eds) *Humanities in the Primary School.* Lewes: Falmer Press.

Lomas, T. (1994) *A Guide to Preparing the History Curriculum in Primary Schools for an OFSTED Inspection.* London: The Historical Association.

Marbeau, L. (1988) 'History and Geography in School', in *Primary Education 88,* Vol. xx. No. 2.

Martin, D. and Cobb, A. (1992) 'Evacuation Day', in *Primary History,* No. 2. London: The Historical Association.

Martin, R. B. (1980) *Tennyson, The Unquiet Heart.* Oxford: Oxford University Press.

Merriman, N. (1990) Curator, Museum of London in *The Times,* 23 August 1990.

Mink, L.O. (1968) 'Collingwood's Dialectic of History', in *History and Theory.* Vol. vii, No. 1.

Mitchell, R. and Middleton. G. (1967) *Living History Book One.* Holmes McDougall.

National Curriculum for History, Final Report (1990).

NCC (1990) *Curriculum Guidance* 6. York: National Curriculum Council.

NCC (1991) *Implementing National Curriculum History.* York: National Curriculum Council.

NCC (1992) *History at Key Stage 2: An Introduction to the Non-European Study Units.* York: National Curriculum Council.

NCC (1993a) *Teaching History at Key Stage 1.* York: National Curriculum Council.

NCC (1993b) *Teaching History at Key Stage 2.* York: National Curriculum Council.

Noble, P. (1986) *The 17th Century.* Sussex: Ward Lock Educational.

Oakes, L. (1994) *The Assyrians,* Bringing History to Life Series, No. 6. London: The Historical Association.

Oliver, D. (1985) 'Language and Learning History', in *Education 3–13.* Vol. 13, No. 1.

Opie, I. and Opie, P. (eds) (1973) *The Oxford Book of Children's Verse.* Oxford: Clarendon.

Osler, A. (1995) 'Does the National Curriculum bring us any Closer to a Gender Balanced History?', in *Teaching History,* 79. London: The Historical Association.

Palmer, M. and Batho, G. (1981) 'The Source Method in History Teaching', *Teaching History Series.* The Historical Association, No. 48.

Parnes, S. H, (1959) 'Instructors Manual for Semester Courses in Creative Problem-Solving', Creative Education Foundation. Buffalo, New York.

Index

Peel, E. A. (1960) *The Pupil's Thinking.* Oldbourne T.

Peel, E. A. (1967) in M. H. Burston and D. Thompson (eds) *Studies in the Nature and Teaching of History.* London: Routledge.

Phenix, P. (1964) *Realms of Meaning.* London and New York: McGraw Hill.

Piaget, J. (1926) (3rd Edn 1959) *The Language and Thought of the Child.* London: Routledge.

Piaget, J. (1928) *Judgement and Reasoning in the Child.* London: Kegan Paul.

Piaget, J. (1932) *Moral Judgement and the Child.* London: Kegan Paul.

Piaget, J. (1950) *The Psychology of Intelligence.* London: Routledge and Kegan Paul.

Piaget, J. and Inhelder, B. (1951) *The Origin of the Idea of Chance in the Child.* London: Routledge.

Piaget, J. (1952) *The Child's Conception of Number.* London: Routledge.

Piaget, J. (1956) *A Child's Conception of Time.* London: Routledge.

Pocock, T. (1974) *Nelson and His World.* London: Thames and Hudson.

Pocock, T. (1987) *Horatio Nelson.* London: Bodley Head.

Plowden Report (1967) Children and their Primary Schools. Report of the Central Advisory Council for Education (England). London: HMSO.

Pounce, E. (1995) 'Ensuring Continuity and Understanding through the Teaching of Gender Issues in History 5–16', in R. Watts and I. Grosvenor (eds) *Crossing the Key Stages of History.* London: David Fulton.

Pring, R. (1976) *Knowledge and Schooling.* Wells: Open Books.

Prisk, T. (1987) 'Letting Them Get On With It: A Study of an Unsupervised Group Task in an Infant School', in A. Pollard *Children and their Primary Schools.* Lewes: Falmer Press.

Rees, A. (1976) 'Teaching Strategies for the Advancement and Development of Thinking Skills in History'. Unpub. MPhil Thesis. University of London.

Richmond, I. A. (1955) *Roman Britain.* Harmondsworth: Penguin.

Richmond, J. (1982) *The Resources of Classroom Language.* London: Arnold.

Roberts, F. (1992) *India 1526–1800.* London: Hodder and Stoughton.

Rodney, W. (1972) *How Europe Underdeveloped Africa.* London: L'Ouverture Bogle.

Rogers, R. C. (1959) 'Towards a Theory of Creativity', in H. H. Anderson (ed.) *Creativity and its Cultivation.* Harper.

Rosen, C. and Rosen, H. (1973) *The Language of Primary School Children.* Harmondsworth: Penguin.

Rowbotham, S. (1973) *Hidden from History.* London: Pluto.

Rowse, A. L. (1946) *The Use of History.* London: Hodder and Stoughton.

Ruddock, J. (1979) *Learning to Teach Through Discussion.* C.A.R.E. University of East Anglia.

Russell, J. (1981) 'Why "Socio-Cognitive Conflict" May be Impossible: The Status of Egocentric Errors in the Dyadic Performance of a Spatial Task', in

Education Psychology 1, pp. 159–69.

Ryle, G. (1979) *On Thinking*. Oxford: Blackwell.

SCAA (1994) *The Impact of the National Curriculum on the Production of History Textbooks at Key Stage 2 and 3.*

SCAA (1995) *Planning the Curriculum at Key Stages 1 and 2.*

Schools Council (1976–1978) *History 13–16*. Edinburgh: Holmes McDougall.

Schools Council (1979) *Learning through Talking 11–16*. London:Evans/ Methuen Educational.

Schools Council (1975–1980) *History, Geography and Social Studies (8–13): Place, Time and Society*. London: Collins ESL.

Schools Council (1983) *Akbar and Elizabeth*. Schools Council Publications.

SEAC (1993) *Children's Work Assessed: History and Geography.*

Sellars, W. C. and Yeatman, R. J. (1973) 1066 and all That. Harmondsworth: Penguin.

Shawyer, G., Booth, M. and Brown, R. (1988) 'The Development of Children's Historical Thinking', in *Cambridge Journal of Education*, Vol. 18, No. 2.

Shemilt, D. (1980) *History 13–16 Evaluation Study*. Edinburgh: Holmes McDougall.

Shif, Zh. (1935) *The Development of Scientific and Everyday Concepts*. Moscow: Uchpedgiz.

Speed, P. and Speed, M. (1987) *The Elizabethan Age, Books 1–4*. Oxford: Oxford University Press.

Smith, L.N. and Tomlinson, P. (1977) 'The Development of Children's Construction of Historical Duration', in *Educational Research*. Vol. 19, No.3, pp. l63–70.

Smith, N. (1992) *Black Peoples of the Americas*. Oxford: Oxford University Press.

Stones, E. (1979) *Psychopedagogy*. (Ch.9). London and New York: Methuen.

Strong, R. (1987) *Glorianna, The Portraits of Queen Elizabeth*. London: Thames and Hudson.

Sylvester, D. (1989) 'Children as Historians', in J. Campbell and V. Little (eds.) *Humanities in the Primary School*. Lewes: Falmer Press.

Tanner, G. and Wood, T. (1993) *Bathtime*. London: A. and C. Black.

Thomas, K. (1983) *Man and the Natural World*. London: Allen Lane.

Thornton, S. J. and Vukelich, R. (1988) 'The Effects of Children's Understanding of Time Concepts or Historical Understanding', *Theory and Research in Social Education*, Winter.

The Times Atlas of Ancient Civilizations (1989) Times Books/The Times.

Tonge, N. (1993) 'Communicating History', in *Teaching History*, 71.

Torrance, E. P. (1962) *Guiding Creative Talent*. London and New York: Prentice Hall.

Torrance, E. P. (1965) *Rewarding Creative Behaviour*. London and New York: Prentice Hall.

Uttley, A. (1977) *A Traveller in Time*. Harmondsworth: Puffin.

Unstead, R. J. (1964) *From Cavemen to Vikings*. London: A. and C. Black Ltd.

Vishram, R. (1988) *Ayars Lascars and Princes*. London: Pluto.

Vygotsky, L. S. (1962) *Thought and Language*. Edited and translated by E. Hanfmann and G. Vakar. London and New York: Wiley.

Wade, B. (1981) 'Assessing Pupils' Contributions in Appreciating a Poem', in *Journal of Education for Teaching* Vol. 7, No. 1, pp.40–9.

Wallach, M. A. and Kagan, N. (1965) *Modes of Thinking in Young Children*. London: Holt, Rinehart and Winston.

Watts, D. G. (1972) *The Learning of History*. London: Routledge and Kegan Paul.

Watts, R. and Grosvenor, I. (eds) (1995) *Crossing the Key Stages of History*. London: David Fulton.

Wedgwood, C. V. (1955) *The King's Peace 1637-1641* (The Great Rebellion). London: Collins.

Wedgwood, C. V. (1958) *The King's War 1641-1647*. London: Collins.

Werner, H. and Kaplan, E. (1963) *Symbol Formation, an Orgasmic Developmental Approach to Language and Expression of Thought*. London and New York: Wiley.

West, J. (1981) 'Children's Awareness of the Past', Unpub. PhD Thesis. University of Keele.

Wood, D. and Middleton, D. (1975) 'A Study of Assisted Problem-Solving', in *British Journal of Psychology*. Vol. 66, pp. 181–91.

Wright, D. (1984) 'A Small Local Investigation', in *Teaching History* No. 39. The Historical Association.

Wright, M. (1992) *A Really Practical Guide to Primary History*. Cheltenham: Stanley Thornes.

RESOURCES REFERRED TO IN THE TEXT

The Association for the Study of African, Caribbean and Asian Culture in Britain, c/o ICS, 27–28 Russell Square, London, WC1

BBC Broadcasting Support Services, PO Box 7, London, W3 6XJ.

Benin: pictures from an African Kingdom (1992), British Museum Education Service, Great Russell Street, London, WC1.

Benin Source Pack for Key Stage 2 (1992), Northamptonshire Black History Group, from Wellingborough REC, Victorian Centre, Park Road, Wellingborough, Northants, NN8 1HT.

British Museum Education Service, Great Russell Street, London, WC1.

English Heritage Education Service, Keysign House, 429 Oxford Street, London.

Eureka Benin: An African Kingdom; video, teacher's resource booklet, poster; Educational Television Co., PO Box 100, Warwick, CV34 6TZ.

The National Trust, 36 Queen Anne's Gate, London, SW1

Women's History Network, Key Stage 1, Biography Project, Department of History, University of York

Index